토익토플 R/C

Hanol Publishing

토 익　토익의 구성　평가기준　토 플　토플의 구성　응시방법

1. TOEIC이란 무엇인가?

TOEIC은 Test of English for International Communication의 약어로 국제적 의사 소통 능력을 측정하기 위한 영어 시험이다. TOEIC의 문제 작성 및 채점은, 미국의 New Jersey에 본부를 둔 ETS(Educational Testing Service)가 시행하고 있다. TOEIC의 최초 테스트는 1979년 12월에 일본에서 실시되었다. TOEFL(Test of English as a Foreign Language)이 미국의 대학에 진학하기 위한 영어 능력 테스트라면 TOEIC은 기업체의 사원이나 일반인들의 영어 능력을 평가하기 위해서 이용되고 있다. 따라서 생활 영어나 비즈니스 영어가 주축을 이루고 있다. TOEIC의 큰 특징은 TOEFL과 마찬가지로 합격, 불합격을 결정하는 것이 아니라 시험 결과가 점수로 표시된다. 우리 나라에서는 1982년 1월에 처음 시행되었고, 요즈음은 대기업 및 중소기업의 신입사원 선발과 승진 심사는 물론 각종 국가고시에도 영어시험을 TOEIC 성적으로 대체하고 있다.

2. TOEIC의 구성

- Listening Test
  PART Ⅰ ················· Sentences About Photographs(사진 묘사 문제) 10문항
  PART Ⅱ ································· Stimuli-Responses(응답 문제) 30문항
  PART Ⅲ ····························· Short Conversations(회화 문제) 30문항
  PART Ⅳ ································· Short Talks(설명문 문제) 30문항

- Reading Test
  PART Ⅴ ···················· Sentence Completion(문법·어휘 문제) 40문항
  PART Ⅵ ···················· Passage Completion(문단완성 문제) 12문항
  PART Ⅶ ···················· Reading Comprehension(독해 문제) 48문항

∴ 실제 시험 시간은 Listening Test에 45분, Reading Test에 75분이 배분된다.

3. TOEIC의 평가 기준

수 준	TOEIC	평 가
A	860점 이상	Non-Native로서 충분한 커뮤니케이션을 할 수 있다. 자기가 경험한 범위 내에서는 전문 분야 이외의 화제에 대해서도 충분한 이해와 적절한 표현을 할 수 있다. Native Speaker의 경지에는 다소 못 미친다할지라도 어휘, 문법, 구문의 어느 것이든 정확히 파악하고, 유창하게 구사할 수 있는 능력을 갖고 있다.
B	860~730점	어떠한 상황에서도 적절한 커뮤니케이션을 할 수 있는 소지를 갖추고 있다. 보통 회화는 완전히 이해하고, 응답도 빠르다. 화제가 특수 분야에 미치더라도 대응할 수 있는 능력을 지니고 있다. 업무상으로도 큰 지장이 없다. 정확하냐 하는 점과, 유창하냐 하는 점에는 개인차가 있으며, 문법 구문 상의 오류가 발견되는 일도 있으나, 의사소통을 방해할 정도는 아니다.
C	729~470점	일상생활에 필요한 것을 충족하고, 한정된 범위 내에서는 업무상의 커뮤니케이션을 할 수 있다. 보통 회화라면 요점을 이해하고, 응답에도 지장이 없다. 복잡한 경우에 있어서의 적절한 대응이나 의사소통은 사람에 따라서 잘하고 못하는 차이가 있다. 기본적인 문법 구문을 익히고 있으며, 표현력은 부족하나마 일단은 자기의 의사를 전달하는 어휘력을 갖추고 있다.
D	469~220점	보통 회화에서 최소한의 커뮤니케이션을 할 수 있다. 천천히 말해 주거나, 되풀이 또는 딴 말로 바꾸어 말해 주면, 간단한 회화는 이해할 수 있다. 친숙한 화제라면 응답도 가능하다. 어휘, 문법, 구문이 모두 불충분한 점이 많으나, 상대가 Non-Native에게 특별한 배려를 해주는 경우에는 의사소통이 될 수 있다.
E	220점 이하	커뮤니케이션을 할 수 있는 단계에 이르지 못했다. 단순히 회화를 천천히 말해도 부분적으로 이해 못한다. 단편적으로 단어를 늘어놓을 뿐, 실질적으로 의사소통에는 도움을 못 준다.

4. 토플

토플(TOEFL: Test of English as a Foreign Language)은 미국 교육평가원(ETS: Educational Testing Service)에서 주관하는 영어시험으로 영어를 모국어로 하지 않은 학생들이 대학 환경에서 사용되는 영어를 얼마나 잘 사용하고 이해하는지를 평가한다. 미국 대학이나 대학원을 희망하는 사람들이라면 거의 필수적으로 치러야 하는 영어시험이다. 인쇄된 문제지와 OMR답지를 사용하는 PBT(Paper Based Test)에서 컴퓨터를 이용하여 수험생의 실력에 따라 다른 난이도의 문제가 출제되는 CBT(Computer Based Test)로 전환되었다가 현재는 통합형 문제를 출제하는 인터넷을 이용한 iBT(Internet Based Test) 형식으로 평가한다.

5. 토플의 구성

영역	점수	시간	문항수	지문
Reading	0 - 30	60 - 100	36 - 70	독해 지문 3-5개 한 지문에 12-14문항
Listening	0 - 30	60 - 90	34 - 54	대화지문 2-3개 3분 길이 한 지문당 5문항 강의지문 4-6개 3분 길이 한 지문당 6문항
		10		휴식시간
Speaking	0 - 30	20	6	독립형 2개 개인선호 의견 진술 통합형 4개 캠퍼스상황, 학술적 주제 요약
Writing	0 - 30	50	2	통합형 1개 지문을 듣고 요약 독립형 1개 하나의 주제에 대한 찬반입장
	0 - 120	약4시간		

6. 응시방법

■ 토플
  인터넷 등록 ETS 등록 사이트(www.toefl.com)

■ 토익
  인터넷 신청
  YBM 시사토익 인터넷 접수를 통해 일정과 장소를 선택할 수 있다.

CONTENTS

PART 1

• • •

실용 연습

01

Welcome to the inflight "Sky Shopping". We offer you a worldwide selection of duty-free items such as liquor, cigarettes, perfumes, cosmetics, chocolates and accessories, etc. These are purchased directly from the manufacturers to secure the lowest possible prices. The information regarding the exchange rate is available in the catalogue in front of your seat pocket. For further information, please ask the cabin attendants. You may purchase any duty free items with the following credit cards; Master Card, VISA, Diners Club International and American Express. Occasionally, due to limited cabin space, certain items may not be loaded or may be sold out. Please accept our apologies if you are unable to purchase any item featured in this guide. Thank you.

어휘

- **inflight**: happening or provided during a trip by plane (기내의, 비행중의)
  - 예문 What's the inflight meal today? (오늘 기내식은 무엇입니까?)

- **liquor**: spirits or any distilled alcoholic drink (brandy, whisky 등의 독주)
  - 예문 Do you have any liquor or cigarettes to declare?
  - (세관에 신고할 양주나 담배를 가지고 계십니까?)

- **secure**: to get, especially as the result of effort (확보하다, 획득하다)
  - 예문 Thet have struggled to secure the freedom of speech.
  - (그들은 언론의 자유를 얻기 위하여 분투했다.)

- **occasionally**: sometimes, once in a while (가끔, 때때로)
  - 예문 I'm not a heavy drinker, but occasionally I like to drink.
  - (나는 술고래는 아니지만 가끔 한잔 하는 것은 좋아한다.)

- **accept**: to take or receive something, especially willingly (받아들이다)
  - 예문 He asked her to marry him and she accepted his offer.
  - (그의 결혼 요청을 그녀는 받아 들였다.)

- **apology**: a statement expressing that one is sorry for having done something wrong, for causing pain or trouble (사과, 사죄)
  - 예문 Please accept our apologies for any inconvenience we have caused.
  - (저희로 인해 야기된 불편한 점에 대하여 사과의 말씀을 드립니다.)

- **owing to~**: (1) ~때문에(on account of)

  예문 Owing to a heavy snowfall the train was delayed.(폭설 때문에 기차가 연착되었다.)

  (2) ~에 의한, ~에 기인한(due to)

  예문 His fame is owing to his own efforts.(그의 명성은 그 자신의 노력에 의한 것이다.)

02

Some of the ideas on the road ; Hyundai, starting around $8,000.

With power steering wheel, tinted glass, automatic transmission and dual airbags, $10,635. The above is exclusive of freight, taxes and other optional items.

Airbags are a supplemental restraint system. So, remember to buckle up everyone.

5 MPH energy-absorbing bumpers that exceed federal requirements. Energy-absorbing front and rear crumple zones. Side impact beams that meet federal safety standards for 2007. Reinforced passenger cabin designed to help disperse the impact energy. ABS for evading the unforeseen.
New technology. New designs. New standards.

To download more information visit us at www.hyundaiUSA.com or call 1 (800) 826 -CARS.

어휘

- **tint**: to give a slight or delicate colour to (엷게 색을 칠하다)

  예문 He bought a nice sports car with tinted glass in all the windows.
  (그는 색유리가 부착된 멋진 스포츠 카 한 대를 구입했다.)

- **supplementary**: additional or extra (보충의, 추가의, 보조의)

  예문 There is a supplementary water supply in case the main supply fails.
  (주요 용수공급장치의 고장에 대비한 보조장치가 준비되어 있다.)

- **crumple**: crushing something into folds or creases (구김살)

예문 The crumple zones are designed to absorb the impact completely.
(크럼플 존은 충격을 완전히 흡수하도록 설계되었다.)

- **disperse**: to scatter or to make somebody/something go in different directions
  (분산시키다, 흩뜨리다, 해산시키다)

  예문 Police used tear gas to disperse the crowd.
  (군중을 해산시키려고 경찰은 최루가스를 사용했다.)

- **evade**: to escape or avoid meeting somebody/something(피하다, 면하다, 벗어나다)

  예문 Give me a direct answer, and stop evading the issue.
  (쟁점을 회피하지 말고 똑바로 말해 주세요.)

- **unforeseen**: not known in advance, unexpected (뜻하지 않은, 우연한)

  예문 Due to unforeseen circumstances the opening has been delayed.
  (뜻하지 않은 사정으로 인하여 개업이 지연되었다.)

- **surpass**: to do or be better than somebody/something (능가하다, 뛰어나다)

  예문 The results surpassed all our expectations.(그 결과는 전혀 우리 예상 밖이었다.)

03

Universal Studio is a lot of fun, combining the best of a "movie studio" attraction with the high-tech rides. A day at Universal Studio is filled with spine-chilling rides, thrilling shows, awesome special effects and amazing adventures. Inside the world's largest studio you'll also see hundreds of sets from your favorite films and TV shows such as Jurassic Park and Back To The Future. You can also experience earthquake terror inside a detailed re-creation of a modern subway station. In slightly more than two minutes, the earth literally collapses, trapping you in a murky nether world of fallen telephone poles, sparking power cables and noxious gases. Furthermore, you can have a chance to meet the world's largest animated figure, King Kong. He's so close, you can feel his hot breath as he begins to snap the bridge's suspension cables, which sends you into a wild slide.

In summer season they open 8:00 a.m. to 10:00 p.m. and non-summer season, 9:00 a.m. to 7:00 p.m.

○ **ride**: an amusement at a fair, which people pay to sit or stand on for a short time while it moves round fast, swings from side to side
(타고 노는 기구, 놀이기구)

例文 You can experience the high-tech rides in Universal Studio

○ **spine-chilling**: spine-tingling, frightening in an exciting way
(등골이 오싹하는, 가슴 두근거리는)

例文 My younger brother likes a spine-chilling ghost story.
(내 동생은 무시무시한 유령 이야기를 좋아한다.)

○ **literally**: really, actually, exactly (정말로, 실제로, 문자그대로)

例文 He was literally blazing with anger. (그는 몹시 화가나 있었다.)

○ **murky**: dark and unpleasant (매우 어두운, 캄캄한, 음울한, 침침한)

例文 Yesterday there was a lot of murky fog at the airport.

○ **noxious**: harmful, poisonous (유해한, 유독한)

例文 Nowadays you can find some noxious chemicals in the river water.
(요즈음 강물에서 몇몇 유해한 화학물질이 발견되기도 한다.)

○ **snap**: to take or obtain with a quick bite or grab
(잡아채다, 손에넣다, 달려들어 물다)

例文 The dog snapped up a piece of meat. (개는 고기토막을 덥석 물었다.)

04

If you are bringing fruits, meats or other agricultural commodities into the United States, you can get through inspection quicker and avoid fines by following a few declaration guidelines. All food items must be declared. Agricultural inspectors will examine fruits, vegatables and plants if they are free of pests or if they can be brought into the country. The fine for not declaring these items is U$100 and must be paid before leaving the inspection line. Fresh, dried, canned meats and other meat products from most foreign countries cannot be brought into the country. There are a few exceptions, so please declare them and ask the inspectors.

Agricultural inspectors are on the look out for those who may be bringing in food items without declaring them. Be safe. You should declare any of those items by checking "YES" on the U.S. Customs Declaration Form - or be prepared to pay a U$100 fine.

- **commodity**: an article of trade or commerce, especially a mineral or farm product (상품, 일용품, 생활필수품)

  예문 There have been big rises in commodities prices.
  (생활필수품 가격이 급등했다.)

- **fine**: an amount of money paid as a punishment (벌금, 과태료)

  예문 One of the best ways to avoid fines is to follow some declaration guidelines.
  (벌금을 물지 않는 가장 좋은 방법중의 하나는 몇가지 신고사항을 지키는 것이다.)

- **examine**: to look at, inquire into, or consider someone/something closely and carefully in order to find out something (조사하다, 검사하다)

  예문 My luggage was closely examined when I entered the country.
  (내 짐은 그 나라 입국시 정밀 검사를 받았다.)

- **declare**: to make a full statement of property for which tax may be owed to the government (세관에 신고하다)

  예문 The customs officer asked me if I had anthing to declare.
  (세관원은 신고할 물건이 없는지 나에게 물었다.)

05

"I didn't think I'd be able to devote myself totally to baseball if I didn't do something to help," says Chanho Park as he explained what brought him to donate 100 Million won to groups helping the children of the recently unemployed. Park returned last Saturday, Jan.9, 1999 to Los Angeles, where he pitches for the LA Dodgers baseball team. "While here in Seoul it really hit me to see so many unemployed living in the area around Seoul Station." Park has made several large donations over the past few years and has made contributions to the Park Chanho Scholarship Foundation in 1997. "I'm in good physical condition right now, but since I participated in the Asian Games during the off season I need to rebuild my strength," he says. "The Dodgers are in good condition as a team at the moment, and I think we have a chance at the World Series."

어휘

- **devote**: to give wholly or completely to (헌신하다, 바치다, 내맡기다)

  예문 He has devoted his life to helping blind people.
  (그는 지금까지 맹인을 돕는 일에 헌신해 왔다.)

- **donate**: to make a gift of something, especially for a good purpose
  (기증하다, 기부하다)

  예문 Last year he donated $10,000 to cancer reserch.
  (지난해 그는 암 연구를 위해 만불을 기부했다.)

- **hit**: to have a bad effect on~(~에 강한 영향을 끼치다, 타격을 가하다)

  예문 The increase in food prices hits everyone's pocket.
  (식품가격의 상승으로 모든 사람들이 고통을 받고 있다.)

- **rebuild**: to build again or build new parts to(재건하다, 개축하다, 보강하다)

  예문 The house was rebuilt after the fire.
  (그 집은 화재로 재건축 되었다.)

06

The 'EURO' which will come into operation at 12:01 a.m. on January 1st, 1999 is historic in that it is the final stage in the formation of a United States of Europe. It also indicates a possible shift in the axis of world economic power, currently centered in the US following the collapse of Russia, and the coming of a bipolarity in economic leadership. The 'EURO' will harmonize and improve trade and industrial competitiveness to produce a strong Europe, backed by a highly educated workforce, technological excellence, and a superior management ability. At the moment Europe occupies 20% of the world's GDP, but with a industrial restructuring and mobile manpower we'll see this drastically expand. Asian countries will now face a stronger newer competition. Japan, which had been trying to expand the yen block in Asia, and the US who currently dominates the markets will see their influence reduced. Unless something unexpected happens the world is about to enter an era with a bi-polar currency system. There is no way to forecast how this will contribute to the stabilization of the world economy, but optimism on a strong Europe backing it up is on the increase. Korea has to reorganize its overseas strategy for these changes. Dependency on US dollars has to be lowered and the country should prepare for increased trade pressure from the Americans as the dollar weakens.

어휘

○ **operation**: the condition or process of working, an activity (운영, 가동, 수술)

> 예문 When does the new law come into operation?
> (그 새로운 법률은 언제 발효됩니까?)

○ **historic**: having or likely to have an influence on history (역사상 중요한)

> 예문 Last Monday there was a historic meeting between two leaders.
> (지난 월요일 두 정상간의 역사적인 회담이 있었다.)

○ **indicate**: to show or make clear, especially by means of a sign

(나타내다, 예시하다, 암시하다)

예문 His reply indicates total disagreement.
(그의 대답은 그가 전혀 찬성하고 있지 않음을 나타낸다.)

● **collapse**: the act of collapsing(falling down as a result of pressure or loss of strength or support) (붕괴, 무너짐, 좌절)

예문 The country's economy is on the verge of collapse.
(그 나라 경제는 붕괴 직전의 상태이다.)

● **mobile**: able to move, or be moved, quickly and easily
(가동성의, 이동하기 쉬운, 유동성이 있는)

예문 She's much more mobile now she has a car.(그녀는 자동차가 있어 기동성이 있다.)

● **drastically**: strongly, suddenly, violently, severely (맹렬히, 철저히)

예문 His work has changed drastically since his illness.
(병든 후 그가 하는 일에 많은 변화가 있었다.)

● **era**: a very long period of time in the history of the earth or of human society, especially as marked by events or developments of a particular kind (시대, 연대, 시기)

예문 The era of space travel has begun. (우주여행 시대가 시작되었다.)

● **optimism**: a tendency to give more attention to the good side of a situation or to expect the best possible result (낙천주의, 낙관)

예문 The antonym of optimism is pessimism.(낙천주의의 반대말은 비관주의이다.)

07

Korea's 2008 Gross National Product(GNP) per capita reversed gears and backed out of the top 40 in the world ranking with 16,321 dollars. However, if the foreign exchange rate remains near its current level it will go up again to the 17,700-dollar mark in 2009. According to the Ministry of Finance and Economics on December 31, this year's growth rate was minus 7 percent which led to the 16,321 dollars per capita GNP. It is far below 2007's 19,511 dollars and even lower than 2001's 16,745 level. Korea's world ranking was 42nd, a considerable fall from last year's 34th and inferior to Malta, Argentina, Puerto Rico, Saudi Arabia and Bahrain. The economic index for 2009 is difficult to predict but some analysts forecast a 2 percent growth rate which would raise the GNP to 17,700 dollars per person. Korea had just passed the 20,000-dollar GNP level in 2005 and 2006 but since the Riman Brother's bankrupsy in the fall of 2007 it has kept moving backwards.

어휘

○ **per capita** (일인당)

capita: a plural form of caput (caput : 머리)

예문 Korea's GNP per capita in 1997 was $9,511.
(1997년 한국의 일인당 GNP는 9,511불이었다.)

○ **reverse**: to go or cause something to go backwards, to change something to the apposite (반대로 하다, 역으로 하다, 뒤집다, 뒤엎다)

예문 Their positions are now reversed.
(그들의 입장은 이제 뒤바뀌었다.)

○ **back out** (퇴각하다, 약속을 파기하다, 벗어나다)

예문 I hope I can depend on you not to back out af the last moment.
(마지막 순간까지 당신이 약속을 파기하지 않는다고 믿고 싶소.)

○ **current**: belong to the present time, of the present day (현재의, 지금의)

예문 Rumors were current about him.
(그 사람에 대해서 여러 가지 소문이 돌고 있다.)

○ **considerable**: fairly large or great (상당한, 적지 않은)

예문 Last year he earned a considerable sum of money.
(지난해 그는 상당한 액수의 돈을 벌었다.)

○ **inferior**: lower in position (낮은, 하급의, 하위의, 열등한)

예문 This novel of his is inferior to the previous one.
(이번에 쓴 그의 소설은 먼저 작품보다 못하다.)

○ **predict**: to see or describe something in advance as a result of knowledge, experience or thought (예상하다, 예언하다, 예견하다)

예문 According to the weather forecast, it's predicted that a storm is coming.
(일기예보에 의하면, 폭풍우가 오는 것을 예보하고 있다.)

○ **forecast**: to predict or to say, especially with the help of some kind of knowledge what is going to happen at some future time
(예보하다, 예측하다, 예상하다)

예문 The teacher forecast that only fifteen of his pupils would pass the exam.
(선생님은 학생중 15명만이 시험에 합격하리라고 예상한다.)

ⓞ **bailout**: help given, especially financially to some organization which is in difficulty (긴급구조, 낙하산 탈출)

예문 The president was hoping for a bailout to save the company.
(사장은 회사 부도를 막기 위한 긴급구조 자금을 바라고 있었다.)

ⓞ **bail**: money left with a court of law so that a prisoner can be set free until he/she is tried (보석금)

예문 She was released on bail of $10,000.(그녀는 보석금 만불에 석방되었다.)

08

Five, four, three, two, one! Happy New Year! It is twelve o'clock midnight. The year ends. A new one begins. Some people are happy. Some people are sad. Everyone thinks about the past year and the next year. New Year's Eve is December 31. It is the night before New Year's Day. People try to be with friends and family. They do not want to be alone. Many people go to parties or restaurants. They eat, drink and dance. At midnight, people ring bells and blow horns. People say, "Happy New Year!" They kiss and hug. January 1 is New Year's Day. It is a national holiday. People do not work. They stay at home. Many Americans watch television on New Year's Day. In the morning, they watch the Tournament of Roses Parade. Everything in the parade has flowers. After the parade, they watch college football games. On New Year's Day, many Americans decide to change their bad habits. Some people promise to spend less money. Some promis to eat less food. But most people forget their promises.

ⓞ **blow**: to send out a strong current of air, especially from the lungs(불다, 울리다)
예문 The wind is blowing from the east. (동쪽에서 바람이 불어오고 있다.)

- **hug**: to hold someone tightly in the arms, especially as a sign of love (포옹하다)

  예문 He hugged his long-missed fiancee.(그는 오랫동안 그리던 약혼녀를 껴안았다.)

- **parade**: a gathering together in ceremonial order, for the purpose of being officially looked at or for a march (행렬, 열병, 퍼레이드)

  예문 The soldiers were on parade in front of City Hall yesterday.
  (어제 시청 앞에서 군인들이 줄지어 행진했다.)

- **decide**: to make a choice or judgment; make up one's mind (결심하다, 결정하다)

  예문 She has decided to become a teacher.
  = She has decided she will become a teacher. (그녀는 교사가 되기로 결심했다.)

- **habit**: an example of customary behaviour (습관, 버릇, 습성, 습관적 행위)

  예문 She is in the habit of drinking. (그녀는 음주벽이 있다.)
  He is in the habit of sitting up late. (그는 밤늦게까지 안 자는 버릇이 있다.)

- **promise**: a statement, which someone else has a right to believe and depend on, that one will or will not do something or give something(약속, 계약, 약속한 것)

  예문 If you make a promise, you should keep it; you ought not to break a promise.
  (약속을 하면 반드시 지켜야 한다; 약속을 절대로 어겨서는 안된다.)

09

Ladies and gentlemen.

The local time is nine o'clock in the morning. For your own safety, please remain seated until the captain has turned off the seat belt sign. Be careful when opening the overhead bins, and check that you have not left any items behind. All portable electronic devices must be turned off until the aircraft is completely parked at the gate. If you have onward or return booking with Air Canada, please reconfirm your flight at least 72 hours before your departure. We thank you for choosing Air Canada and we hope to see you again soon. Thank you for flying with us today and we wish you a pleasant stay here in Vancouver. Thank you.

remain: to stay or be left behind after others have gone or been removed

(남다, 머무르다, 체제하다, 변함없이 그대로이다)

예문 They remained at peace. (그들은 여전히 평화스러웠다.)

Let it remain as it is. (그것을 그대로 내버려두시오.)

turn off: to stop a radio, television or light by using a button or switch (끄다)

예문 Tom, why don't you turn off the television? It's too late.

(Tom, 텔레비젼 좀 꺼 주겠니? 너무 늦었어.)

bin: a large storage container, especially one with a lid; compartment (선반, 짐 칸)

예문 Be careful when you open the overhead bins on the plane.

(기내에서 머리 위 선반을 열 때에는 조심하세요.)

portable: that can be easily carried or moved; quite small and light (휴대용의, 간편한)

예문 All portable electronic devices must be turned off during the flight.

(비행 중 모든 휴대용 전자제품의 사용은 금지된다.)

device: a piece of equipment intended for a particular purpose (장치, 고안물, 제품)

예문 The missile has a heat-seeking device which enables it to find its target.

(그 미사일에는 열 추적 장치가 부착되어 있어 목표물을 추적할 수 있다.)

booking: a case or the act of booking a seat or hotel room; reservation (예약)

예문 She bought a flight ticket at the booking office in Seoul.

(그녀는 서울에 있는 예약 사무소에서 비행기표를 샀다.)

10

For the last five years I have been working at Yoori International Trading Company as an Import & Export Manager. I am currently looking for a job that would widen my experience in the much more competitive business field like your company. I graduated from the Department of Economics, Halla University in 2005 and then, I got a Master's of Business Administration at the same university in 2009. On leaving Halla University I have worked for Yoori International Trading Company up to now. My five years of continuous international trading experience have taught me how to do all phrases of office work. Therefore, the position which offers an opportunity to utilize my potential ability in your company would be very great for me. I sincerely hope that my qualifications are of interest to you and that an interview might be arranged at your earliest convenience.

어휘

- **competitive**: eager to be more successful than other people
  (남에게 지지 않는, 경쟁의, 경쟁심이 강한)
  예문 Our firm is no longer competitive in world markets.
  (우리 회사는 더 이상 세계 시장에서 경쟁력이 없다.)

- **continuous**: continuing without interruption; unbroken (끊임없는, 부단한, 계속적인)
  예문 The government is under continuous pressure to reform the parliamentary system. (정부는 의회제도 개선에 대한 지속적인 압력을 받고 있다.)

- **offer**: to provide; give (제공하다, 제안하다, 제출하다, 내놓다)
  예문 He offered his opinion on this matter. (그는 이 문제에 관한 의견을 제출했다.)

- **utilize**: to make good use of~(~에 이용하다, 활용하다)
  예문 It is to be hoped that in her new job her talents will be better utilized than before. (그녀가 새로 얻은 직장에서 과거보다 더 나은 실력 발휘가 기대된다.)

- **potential**: that may happen, although not actually existing at present (잠재력이 있는)
  예문 He has a potential orator. (그는 웅변가로서 소질이 있는 사람이다.)
  She has a potential oratress. (그녀는 웅변가로서 소질이 있는 사람이다.)

- **convenience**: the quality of being convenient; an apparatus or service which gives comfort or advantage to its user (편리함, 형편이 좋은 상태)
  예문 You may come at any time that suits your convenience.
  (언제든 형편 좋으실 때 오시면 됩니다.)

11

The term 'tip' originated in a London coffee house in a busy street where Samuel Johnson, a very famous writer, and his friends frequently visited during the eighteenth century. On the table was a bowl with the words, 'To Insure Promptitude', printed around it. The phrase was later shortened to 'TIP', taking the first letter of each of the three words. Today, a person is expected to leave a tip even though the service has been slow and indifferent. The unfairness of the custom of tipping, as far as the customer is concerned, depends on the feeling that he is being pressured into carrying part of the employer's burden. If he pays a good price for his haircut, why should he tip the barber? Isn't it up to the employer to provide an adequate wage for him? Or, when he stays in a hotel and pays that bill, why should he give the maid extra money for coming in to clean his room? Isn't it a duty of hotel management to pay her a sufficient salary?

- **term**: a word or expression that has a particular meaning or is used in a particular activity, job or profession (용어, 말, 전문어, 표현)

  예문   The word 'moron' is a term of abuse.('바보'라는 말은 상대방을 모욕하는 말이다.)

- **originate**: to cause to begin; spring; arise (일어나다, 시작되다, 발원하다)

  예문   Coal has originated from the decay of plants.(석탄은 식물이 썩어서 생긴 것이다.)

- **promptitude**: readiness to act; quickness (신속, 기민, 즉결)

  예문   TIP stands for 'To Insure Promptitude.'(팁은 '신속함을 보장한다'는 의미이다.)

- **indifferent**: not very good (그다지 좋지 않은, 평범한, 관심 없는)

  예문   Was it good, bad or indifferent?(좋았습니까, 나빴습니까 아니면 보통이었습니까?)

- **burden**: a heavy duty or responsibility which is hard to bear (짐, 부담, 책임, 의무)

  예문   People on high incomes face a huge tax burden.
  (고소득 계층은 높은 세금 부담에 직면하고 있다.)

- **adequate**: enough for the purpose; having the necessary qualities (적절한, 적당한)

  예문   He is quite adequate to the task.(그는 그 업무에 적임자이다.)

12

Youngpoong Manulife, the most professional life insurance company in Korea is looking for highly qualified and motivated Branch Managers. Founded in 1887, Manulife Financial of Canada provides various life and investment products to clients worldwide. Manulife's service, financial strength and profitability have been recognized for long and proven through excellent ratings by internationally renowned rating agencies such as Moody's and S&P. Especially, Manulife has been successful in Asia for more than 100 years. As a joint venture with Manulife Financial, we believe that now is the time to recruit branch managers for 'The Take-off' of our plan to be the best life insurance company in Korea. For those who want to be part of a growing company, this could be your life time opportunity. To learn more about Manulife Financial, please visit our internet site at www.manulife.com.

어휘

- **insurance**: agreement by contract to pay money to someone if something, especially a misfortune, such as illness, death or an accident happens to them (보험, 보험료, 보험금)

  예문 Does your insurance cover the damage by flooding?
  (가입하신 보험은 홍수로 인한 피해도 보상됩니까?)

- **qualified**: having suitable knowledge or qualifications, especially for a job(자격 있는)

  예문 She is qualified as a teacher of French.
  (그녀는 프랑스어 교사 자격을 갖추고 있다.)

- **motivate**: to provide someone with a strong reason for doing something (동기를 부여하다, 유발하다)

  예문 We have got to try and motivate our salesmen.
  = We have got to make them try harder to sell things.
  (우리는 노력해서 판매사원에게 동기를 부여해야 한다.)

- **profitability**: the state of being profitable or the degree to which a business or operation is profitable (수익성)

  예문 The company hopes to return to profitability this year.

(그 회사는 금년에 흑자가 나기를 기대하고 있다.)

● **renowned**: well known to the general public or to a limited group of people for a particular quality, skill or invention; famous (유명한, 명성 있는)

예문 Edison was a renowned inventor. (Edison은 유명한 발명가였다.)

● **recruit**: to find in order to employ (모집하다, 보충하다, 보강하다, 보급하다)

예문 We are having some difficulties in recruiting qualified English teachers.
(훌륭한 자격을 갖춘 영어 교사를 모집하는데 약간의 애로사항이 있다.)

13

Second language acquisition is a complex process, involving many interrelated factors. Second language acquisition is not a uniform and predictable phenomenon. There is no single way in which learners acquire some knowledge of a second language. Second language acquisition is the product of many factors pertaining to the learner on the one hand and the learning situation on the other. It is important, therefore, to start by recognizing the complexity and diversity that results from the interaction of these two sets of factors. Different learners in different situations learn a second language in different ways.

Second language acquisition stands in contrast to first language acquisition. It is the study of how learners learn an additional language after they have acquired their mother tongue. A theory of second language acquisition is an attempt to show how linguistic input, internal processing, and linguistic output are related.

어휘

● **acquire**: to gain or come to possess, especially by one's own work, skill or action, often over a long period of time (습득하다, 취득하다, 얻다, 배우다)

예문 I managed to acquire two tickets for the concert.
(나는 겨우 그 음악회 입장권 두 장을 구했다.)

● **uniform**: the same all over; not different or varying in any way; regular
　　　　(획일적인, 일률적인, 같은 모양의, 일정한, 변함없는)
　　예문　The recent air-conditioning system maintains a uniform temperature through-
　　　　out the building. (최신 에어콘 시스템으로 건물내의 온도가 일정하게 유지된다.)

● **predictable**: that can be predicted (예측할 수 있는, 예언할 수 있는)
　　예문　To learn a foreign language is not a uniform and predictable phenomenon.
　　　　(외국어를 습득하는 것은 획일적이고 예측할 수 있는 현상이 아니다.)

● **diversity**: the condition of being different or having differences; variety (다양성)
　　예문　There was a considerable diversity of opinion on this issue.
　　　　(이 문제점에 관하여 수많은 다양한 의견이 표출되었다.)

● **interact**: to have an effect on each other or something else by being or working
　　　　close together (상호 작용하다, 서로 영향을 미치다)
　　예문　My son has some difficulty interacting with other children.
　　　　(내 아들은 다른 아이들과 사귀는데 어려움을 느끼고 있다.)

● **linguistic**: of languages, words, or linguistics (언어의, 언어학의, 어학상의)
　　예문　There have been a lot of linguistic studies on the development of Korean language.
　　　　(한국어 발달에 관한 많은 언어학적인 연구가 진행되어 왔다.)

14

When he is very young, a child is usually taught not to lie. He is told that to lie is wrong, to tell the truth is right and there is no in-between. As he grows up, however, it becomes clear that the world is not made up of black and white, but only a series of greys. By the time he reaches adolescence, a boy knows that there are times when it is better to lie (we call it a 'white lie' to rationalize it) than to tell the absolute, unsparing truth. These lies are part of everyday social life, and society would be in an extremely uncomfortable situation without them. Thus people tell other people they look fine, or the new dress is pretty, or they can not come to dinner on a particular night because they are ill, or any one of a thousand other 'white lies', so that the feelings will not be hurt and so that people can live more comfortably together.

> Unless one is a very rigid person, he doesn't feel guilty about telling white lies.

- **lie**: to tell a lie (거짓말을 하다, 속이다)
  - 예문 He managed to lie himself out of difficulties.
    (그는 거짓말을 하여 가까스로 곤경에서 벗어났다.)

- **rationalize**: to find reasons for one's own unreasonable behavior or opinions
  (합리화하다, 합리적으로 설명하다)
  - 예문 She rationalized her fears on the terrible scenes.
    (그녀는 무서운 장면에 대한 두려움을 합리화했다.)

- **absolute**: complete; perfect (절대적인, 온전한, 완전한)
  - 예문 We now have absolute proof of his guilt.
    (그의 잘못에 대한 명백한 증거를 가지고 있다.)

- **unsparing**: holding nothing back, especially money or help; very generous
  (아끼지 않는, 엄한, 가차없는)
  - 예문 In doing anything he is unsparing of himself.
    (어떤 일을 해도 그는 몸을 아끼지 않는다.)

- **rigid**: firm or fixed in behaviour, views or methods (엄격한, 엄중한, 완고한, 단단한)
  - 예문 It is not so easy to keep the rigid discipline of army life.
    (군생활의 엄격한 규율을 지키는 것은 쉬운 일이 아니다.)

- **guilty**: having broken a law or disobeyed a rule (유죄의, 죄를 범한, 범죄의)
  - 예문 The police suspect that the secretary may be the guilty person.
    (경찰은 그 비서를 유력한 용의자로 의심하고 있다.)

15

My name is Grace Kim, living in Seoul. From now, let me introduce my worst experience to you. It happened on an airplane about two years ago. It was in the summer. I was flying from Narita, Tokyo to Vancouver at that time. When the plane took off from Narita, the wind was blowing violently and it was raining hard, too. I was a little nervous. The plane was all right for about three hours after take-off. I was listening to the music on the airplane. Some people were talking to each other or reading newspapers and others were sleeping. The stewardesses were serving drinks to the passengers. Suddenly, however, lightning struck one of the engines. The plane dropped rapidly. Some people were screaming, and the stewardesses were falling down. My heart was beating very fast. I thought I was going to die. But after about thirty or forty seconds, the pilot started the engine again. We landed safely and soundly on the ground. But I will never fly again when the weather is bad.

어휘

- **worst**: the most bad thing or part (최악의, 가장 나쁜, 가장 심한)

  예문 He is the worst person that I have ever known.
  (나는 그 사람처럼 나쁜 사람을 만난 적이 없다.)

- **violent**: very bad or strong (자연 현상·사람의 행동·감정 따위가 맹렬한, 격렬한)

  예문 The demonstrators suddenly turned violent.
  (데모 참가자들은 갑자기 격렬하게 돌변했다.)

- **nervous**: excited and anxious; worried (초조한, 흥분하기 쉬운, 겁이 많은)

  예문 Don't be nervous! The doctor just wants to help you, darling.
  (걱정하지 말아요. 의사 선생님께서 곧 도와주실 거예요, 여보.)

- **rapid**: quick-moving; fast (신속한, 빠른, 급속한, 기민한)

  예문 He asked me a lot of questions in rapid succession.
  (그는 빠른 속도로 계속해서 많은 질문을 나에게 던졌다.)

- **scream**: to cry out loudly on a high note, as in fear, pain, great excitement or anger, or sometimes laughter (비명을 지르다, 소리를 지르다, 낄낄 웃다)

예문 She screamed that her baby was being killed.
(그녀는 자기 아이가 죽는다고 비명을 질렀다.)

○ **sound**: in good condition; without disease or damage (신체·정신이 건강한, 온전한)

예문 A sound mind in a sound bady.(건전한 정신은 건전한 신체에서.)

16

A 16 year-old schoolgirl, Su-In Kim, the youngest person to ever achieve the highest score in Korea scored 990 points at the 79th TOEIC, Test of English for International Communication. She took the test on February 28th, 1999 when she was just a junior-high school student. She scored 495 points both in the listening comprehension section and reading comprehension section. Chief of the computing data department of the TOEIC administration, Mr. Oh said that "45 applicants among 29,400 who took the TOEIC scored 990 points this time and she is the youngest person ever to get the highest." He added that it was rare for junior-high school students to take the TOEIC examination before 1997.

She started to study English with daily study papers when she was a fifth grade student in 1994 and during her stay in Hawaii with her father, an exchange professor at that time, her English ability was accelerated. She said that she always tries to think something in English and keeps an English diary.

She also watches foreign TV channels such as CNN and the Discovery Channel, and reads books written in English to understand foreign cultures, life styles and way of thinking of local people in the world.

○ **achieve**: to get as the result of action; gain (성취하다, 획득하다, 달성하다)

예문 He hopes to achieve all his aims by the end of the year.
(금년 말에는 그의 모든 소원이 이루어지길 희망한다.)

- **comprehension**: the action of understanding (이해, 파악, 이해력)

  (예문) That's beyond my comprehension. (나는 그것을 이해할 수 없다.)

- **chief**: a leader; person with highest rank; head of a party or organization
  (어떤 조직이나 단체의 장, 우두머리, 지도자, 지휘자)

  (예문) Mr. Smith was the chief of police in Las Vegas in 1998.
  (Smith씨는 1998년 당시 Las Vegas 경찰 서장이었다.)

- **rare**: unusual; uncommon (드문, 희귀한, 진귀한)

  (예문) It's very rare for him to be late. (그가 늦는 것은 매우 드문 일이다.)

- **accelerate**: to cause to move faster (촉진하다, 빠르게 하다, 가속하다)

  (예문) The scandal accelerated the fall of the Cabinet. (그 추문은 내각의 붕괴를 앞당겼다.)

17

As you know, Rome is in southern part of Italy, and it is the beautiful and magnificent capital of Italy. It is a very large city and it has about three million people. Rome usually has warm weather because it is close to the Mediterranean Sea. Rome also has a lot of fantastic historic spots to visit. For example, the Vatican, the Colosseum, and the Fountain of Trevi are all in Rome. Rome also has many beautiful parks. Romans like to walk in the parks, and to sit in the comfortable cafes. Every Roman likes to have fun, and Rome is one of the great cities to have fun in the world.

어휘

- **magnificent**: wonderfully fine, grand or excellent (장대한, 화려한, 훌륭한)

  (예문) What a magnificent day (it is)!
  = What a day of very fine weather! (정말 좋은 날씨이군요!)

- **capital**: a town which is the center of government of a country or other
  political unit (수도, 서울; 대문자; 자본, 자본금)

  (예문) Paris is the capital of France. (France 수도는 Paris다.)

- **fantastic**: extremely good or excellent; extraordinarily great (아주 멋진, 훌륭한)

  (예문) What a fantastic meal! (정말 맛있는 음식이군!)

● **historic**: important in history; having or likely to have an influence on history
　　　　　(역사상 중요한, 역사상 유명한)

예문　There was a historic meeting between the great leaders in Washington.
　　　(역사적인 의미를 가진 두 정상간의 회담이 Washington에서 개최되었다.)
　　　You can find a lot of historic sites and tourist attractions in Korea.
　　　(한국에는 유적지와 관광명소가 많이 있다.)

● **historical** : connected with history as a study; based on or representing events
　　　　　in the past (역사적인, 역사에 바탕을 둔)

예문　There was a historical event, KOREAN WAR on June 25, 1950.
　　　(한국전쟁이라는 역사적인 사건이 1950년 6월25일 일어났다.)

18

Belize, which lies on the east coast of Central America, is a former British colony and has a population of approximately two million. The climate of Belize is sub-tropical and the country has an average temperature of twenty centigrade. Running the length of the coastline of Belize is a barrier reef, which is second only in size to the Australian Great Barrier Reef. As well as protecting the coastline from hurricane damage, Belize's barrier reef has always been an essential source of food and income for local fishermen. Like the government of other developing countries, the Belizean government has actively encouraged the development of tourism as a way of earning foreign currency. Last year, over 200,000 tourists visited the country. But the growth of tourism is now threatening the marine life of the coral reef. In order to make room for hotels to be built, the swamps of tropical mangrove trees have had to be cleared. The coral reef itself is also under threat from pollution and from the physical damage caused by the anchors of cruise ships. Additionally, over-fishing has seriously reduced the populations of fish and shellfish such as conch, grouper and lobster.

● **sub-tropical**: semitropical; of or suited to an area near the tropics (아열대의)

예문 The climate of Belize is sub-tropical. (Belize는 아열대성 기후를 띠고 있다.)

● **coral reef**: a mass of limestone, a type of hard rock, formed by coral and/or other living things in warm, shallow sea water and known for its beautiful colours (산호초)

예문 The growth of tourism industry is threatening the marine life of coral reef.
(관광산업의 발달로 인하여 산호초의 해양 생태계가 위협받고 있다.)

● **swamp**: an area land which is always full of or covered with water; marsh (늪)

예문 Some tropical plants are growing in the swamp.(몇몇 열대성 식물이 습지에서 자라고 있다.)

● **essential**: completely necessary for the existence or success of something; central; most important; fundamental; indispensable (필수적인, 본질적인, 절대적인)

예문 Good health is essential to success in life.(인생에 성공하려면 건강은 필수적이다.)

● **pollution**: the action of polluting or the state of being polluted (오염, 공해, 더러움)

예문 Environmental pollution has caused a lot of serious problems in Korea.
(환경오염으로 인하여 한국에서는 많은 문제가 발생되고 있다.)

19

Dear Sirs:

It is a great pleasure to introduce our hotel to you.

Your arrival at the Radisson Seoul Plaza Hotel is welcomed with warmth and smiles. Seoul Plaza is one of Korea's most prestigious hotels, situated in the very heart of Seoul's central business and shopping district, overlooking traditional scenery, the ancient Doksu Palace.

Select from a variety of 480 deluxe guest rooms, a magnificent Royal Suite and exclusive Club Plaza Floors. Complete banquet and catering service can be custom-tailored to suit your need. At our stunning new Grand Ballroom and other Banquet Halls equipped with the most advanced facilities we can accommodate up to 1,000 guests assisted by our experienced banquet personnel.

Sincerely yours,

● **magnificent**: wonderfully fine, grand or excellent (장대한, 훌륭한, 근사한)

　　예문　There are a lot of magnificent tourist attractions in Kyungju City.
　　　　(경주시에는 훌륭한 관광명소가 많이 있다.)

● **custom-tailored**: to be dealt with or done something by one's need or order
　　　　　　　　　(~을 개인의 주문·필요에 따라 다루다)

　　예문　Complete banquet service can be custom-tailored to suit your need.
　　　　(다양한 고객의 욕구를 충족시키기 위한 완벽한 연회 서비스가 제공됩니다.)

● **suit**: to satisfy or please; be acceptable or convenient for (만족시키다, 알맞게 하다)

　　예문　Will it suit you if I come around at three o'clock this afternoon?
　　　　(오늘 오후 3시경 오면 되겠습니까?)
　　　　You may come at any time that suits your convenience.
　　　　(언제든 형편 좋으실 때 오시면 됩니다.)

● **stunning**: splendid; extremely attractive or beautiful(훌륭한, 아름다운, 기절시킬 만한)

　　예문　She looks completely stunning in that dress.
　　　　(그 옷을 입으니 그녀는 정말 멋져 보인다.)

20

★★★ Travelling to the United Kingdom from outside the European Union ☆☆☆

You have to go through customs if you arrive in the United Kingdom after travelling from or through a country that is not in the European Union.

You must declare:

- any goods over the allowances that you have bought in a country that is not in the European Union.
- any prohibited, restricted goods or commercial goods.

If you have something to declare, go to the red point or into the red channel. Only go through the green channel if you are sure that you have no more than the customs allowances and no prohibited, restricted or commercial goods. If you arrive by air and are transferring to a flight to another European Union country, you do not collect your baggage until you reach your final destination. At the transfer point, you only have to declare goods in your cabin baggage. At your final destination, you must declare goods in your hold baggage.

어휘

- **go through**: to pass through or be accepted by (지나가다, 통과하다)

  예문 The proposal must go through several stages to the final settlement.
  (그 제안이 최종적으로 통과되려면 여러 단계를 거쳐야만 한다.)

- **declare**: to make a full statement of property for which tax may be owed to the government (소득액·과세품·휴대품 등을 신고하다)

  예문 Do you have anything to declare? Nothing to declare.
  (신고할 물건이 있습니까? 신고할 것이 없습니다.)

- **allowance**: an amount of money one is allowed to earn free of tax (허용, 승인)

  예문 You must declare any goods over the allowances that you have bought in a foreign country. (일정금액 이상 외국에서 구매한 상품에 대해서는 모두 신고해야만 한다.)

- **prohibit**: to forbid by law or rule; prevent; make impossible (금지하다, 제지하다)

  예문 We are prohibited from drinking alcohol during working hours.
  (저희 회사는 근무시간에 술을 마시는 것을 금지하고 있습니다.)

- **restrict**: to keep within limits of size or number or to a certain limit (제한하다, 한정하다, 법으로 금지하다)

  예문 We had to restrict the number of students on the TOEIC course.
  (우리는 TOEIC 과목에 대한 학생 수를 제한해야만 했다.)

- **commercial**: produced in order to make money, rather than for art (상업적인, 상업상의, 영리적인)

  예문 His new record is too much commercial.
  (그의 새 음반은 상업주의 색채가 농후하다.)

21

◇◇◇◇◇ **Main Street, U.S.A.** ◆◆◆◆◆

Pass through the gates of the Theme Park, Disneyland and enter another world with your first steps on Main Street, U.S.A. Antique automobiles and horse-drawn streetcars move up and down this busy street --- and don't miss the spectacular daily parade! The magic starts as soon as you enter Main Street, U.S.A. and there is at least one fabulous parade every day of the year, with special themes and characters. Steam trains depart Main Street Station for a trip around the Park whilst at the far end of the Street is the Central Plaza.

Occasionally certain rides and facilities may not operate due, for example, to routine maintenance. Please note that certain rides may be unsuitable for pregnant women or people with health problems.

- **antique**: made in an early period and usually valuable (옛 시대의, 고풍스러운)
  - 예문 It's not so easy to buy antique furniture made in the Yi dynasty.
  - (이조 시대에 만들어진 고풍스러운 가구를 구입하기란 쉽지 않다.)

- **spectacular**: attracting excited notice; very impressive; unusually interesting or grand (장관인, 굉장한, 볼만한, 구경거리의)
  - 예문 The drama was a spectacular success in Japan.(그 드라마는 일본에서 크게 성공했다.)

- **fabulous**: marvelous; incredible; excellent; fantastic (믿어지지 않는, 아주 멋진)
  - 예문 It was a fabulous party. (아주 멋진 파티였다.)
  - You're fabulous, Lisa. (Lisa, 넌 최고야!)

- **routine**: regular and habitual way of working or doing things (정기적인 일, 판에 박힌 일, 일과)
  - 예문 She longed to escape from the same tedious routine.
  - (매일같이 반복되는 지겨운 일과에서 벗어나기를 바랬다.)

- **maintenance**: the action of keeping something in good condition (보존, 유지)
  - 예문 Occasionally certain rides may not be operated due to routine maintenance.
  - (때때로 정기 검사로 인하여 어떤 놀이기구는 가동되지 않을 수도 있다.)

◦ **unsuitable**: not adequate or proper; unfit (부적당한, 당치않은, 적임이 아닌)

  예문 Please note that certain rides may be unsuitable for pregnant women.
  (어떤 놀이기구는 임산부에게 해로울지 모르니 유의하시기 바랍니다.)

22

The smoking rate of Korean youngsters was revealed to be the highest in the world, according to a booklet published by the Ministry of Health and Welfare on May 12, 1999. The report showed Korean 18 year-old males in their last year of high-school had a smoking rate of 41.6%, much higher than those of African American counterparts, 28.2% and Japanese seniors, 26.2%.

The smoking rate of Korean high-school girls was 7.3% and although this is much lower than the United Kingdom, 26.5% and the United States, 17.4%. It was higher than Japanese high-school girls, 5.2% and Russian, 4.8%.

◦ **rate**:

(1) a quantity such as value, cost, or speed, measured by its relation to some other amount (비율, 율)

예문 What's the average birth rate in Korea?(한국에서의 평균 출생률은 얼마입니까?)

(2) a charge or payment fixed according to a standard scale (요금, 가격, 시세)

예문 What's the going rate for computer programmers?
= What's the average rate for computer programmers?
(컴퓨터 프로그래머의 평균 급여는 어느 정도입니까?)

◦ **reveal**: to show or allow something previously hidden to be seen
(가리키다, 나타내다, 누설하다, 폭로하다)

예문 The painting reveals the painter.(화풍을 보면 누구 그림인지 알 수 있다.)

◦ **welfare**: well-being; help provided for people with social problem or money difficulties (복리, 복지, 번영, 행복)

예문 The company's welfare division deals with employee's personal problems.
(회사의 복지부에서는 종업원의 개인적인 문제를 다루고 있다.)

○ **counterpart**: a person or thing that has the same purpose or does the same job as another in a different system (상대물, 복사물, 한 쌍의 한쪽)

예문　The counterpart of man is woman. (남자와 짝을 이루는 것은 여자다.)

The Minister of Defence is going to meet his American counterpart in New York tomorrow. (국방부 장관은 내일 New York에서 미국 국방부 장관을 만날 예정이다.)

23

Her Majesty, Queen Elizabeth II left Korea on April 22, 1999, after a four-day visit. Prior to Her Majesty's departure, Queen Elizabeth II visited the British Council, the Anglican Church, and the British Ambassador's Residence.

Highlights of Her Majesty, Queen Elizabeth II were the Queen's Birthday Party in Hahoe Village, Ahn-Dong and the visit to Insa-Dong in downtown Seoul. Thanks to countless rehearsals, the birthday party ended successfully. Bystanders said that the Queen at first seemed a little overwhelmed at the amount of food prepared, but nodded her head when informed that the food was to be shared with all the people in the village. Queen Elizabeth II is said to have been especially impressed by the traditional Korean thatched houses.

어휘

○ **Majesty**: an official title used for addressing or speaking of a king or queen (폐하: 왕, 여왕, 황제, 황후에 대한 경칭으로 소유격과 함께 사용함)

예문　Her Majesty Queen Elizabeth the Second visited Hahoe Village last April. (Elizabeth 여왕 2세는 지난 4월 하회 마을을 방문했다.)

※ Her Imperial Majesty (황후 폐하), His Imperial Majesty (황제 폐하)

The King's Most Excellent Majesty (국왕 폐하)

The Queen's Most Excellent Majesty (여왕 폐하)

○ **rehearsal**: an occasion of rehearsing a play or concert (연극·음악 따위의 시연, 리허설, 예행 연습, 총연습)

예문　This play still needs a lot of rehearsals. (연극을 공연하려면 아직 많은 연습을 해야 한다.)

○ **impress**: (often passive, not in progressive forms) to influence deeply, especially with a feeling of admiration (깊이 감동시키다, 감명을 주다, 인상지우다)

예문 My mother was deeply impressed by my performance in the TOEIC test. (어머니는 내 토익 성적에 깊은 감동을 받았다.)

○ **overwhelm**: (of feelings) to make someone completely helpless, usually suddenly (압도하다, 당황하게 하다, 맥을 못추게 하다)

예문 They overwhelmed me with many embarrassing questions. (당황스러운 질문을 퍼부어 그들은 나를 난처하게 했다.)

24

Many Chinese tourists are heading towards Korea for their golden May Day holiday, Apr. 29 to May 3, 1999. Tourist agencies are having much difficulty in finding vacant airline seats and hotel rooms as twice the normal number of tourists have decided to come to Korea. A tourist agency in Beijing said that "Chinese women are mainly interested in shopping, while the men are more interested in bars or casinos."

Everland in Yongin, Lotte World, Kyungju and Cheju Island are already well-known places for Chinese tourists. The total cost visiting Korea has gone down due to competition; for example, a tour of Seoul and Kyungju for three days costs 3,600 Yuan(500,000 Won). Normally there were about 300 visa cases per day, but for the last ten days, the number has doubled to 600 to 700 cases, and that of tourists travelling in groups has tripled. Since April 29 there have been no air tickets or hotels in Seoul available.

○ **head**: to move in the specified direction (향하다, 진행하다)

예문 Where are you headed? = Where are you heading?(어디 가십니까?)

○ **vacant**: not filled or occupied; empty(토지·방·집·좌석 등이 비어 있는, 공석중인)

예문 Do you have a room vacant? (빈 방 있습니까?)

- **decide**: to make a decision; consider something and come to a conclusion (결정하다)

  예문 It's difficult to decide between the two.
  (둘 중에 어느 것으로 할 지 결정하기 쉽지 않다.)
  With so much choice, it's hard to decide what to buy.
  (선택할 것이 너무 많아 무엇을 사야할 지 잘 모르겠다.)

- **competition**: activity in which people compete; a contest (경쟁, 시합, 경기)

  예문 We're in competition with several other companies for the contract.
  = We're competing against several other companies for the contract.
  (그 계약을 체결하기 위해 우리는 많은 업체와 경쟁하고 있다.)

- **available**: (of things) that can be obtained or used (사용할 수 있는, 유효한)

  예문 This is the ticket available on the day of issue.
  (이것은 발행 당일만 유효한 표입니다.)

25

Korean-American figure skater Naomi Nam is the newest darling of the skating world. She took second place at the most recent United States Figure Skating Championship, which ended Feb.14, 1999. Although skating superstar Michelle Kwan won first place, the LA Times said that Nam was the star of the competition, paying her a high compliment that her performance was full of energy and charisma. The Times announced her arrival on the international skating scene, noting that spectators rose to their feet to give her a standing ovation before her performance was even over and reporting that even the coaches of other competing skaters were thrilled by her excellent performance. Her coach, John Nicks, said that the 13-year old would not take part in the World Championships because of a minimum age requirement.

어휘

- **darling**: a person or thing that is much liked or loved
  (소중한 사람, 가장 사랑하는 사람, 귀여운 사람)

  예문 Pearl Sinn is the darling of the media at the moment.
  (Pearl Sinn는 지금 매스컴으로부터 각광을 받고 있다.)

compliment: an expression of praise, admiration or approval (칭찬, 축하, 치하)

예문 Your presence is a great compliment. (왕림해 주셔서 감사합니다.)

charisma: great charm or personal power that can attract, influence and inspire people (카리스마적 자질, 카리스마적 존재)

예문 General Park was a tremendous popular charisma.
(박 장군은 대단히 인기 있는 카리스마적 자질의 소유자였다.)

spectator: a person who watches a show or game (구경꾼, 관객)

예문 Most spectators rose to their feet to give her a standing ovation before her performance was even over.
(대부분의 관중들은 공연이 끝나기도 전에 일어서서 그녀에게 기립박수를 보냈다.)

ovation: a long and enthusiastic show of appreciation from an audience
(대단한 갈채, 열렬한 환영, 대인기)

예문 The team received an enthusiastic ovation at the airport yesterday.
(그 팀은 어제 공항에서 열렬한 환영을 받았다.)

26

A Korean housewife tourist was freed at 5:30 p.m. on June 25, 1999 after being detained for six days by North Korea for alleged spying during her tour of Mountain Kumgang. She was detained by the North Korean authorities for her trying to convince a local tour guide to defect to the South. The release of Korean tourist was officially announced at 5:00 p.m. in a broadcast on the state-run radio station based in Pyungyang. They announced that she was released in consideration of the country's relations with Hyundai Group, and the South Korean people's desire to see Mountain Kumgang.

For her prompt release, the Korean government and Hyundai spared no effort. When she arrived at Sokcho port in the East Sea aboard a Hyundai's tug-boat, she was almost worn out, so she had to be carried on a stretcher into an ambulance. After returning to Seoul, she was immediately sent to a medical center due to her poor heath condition. Last Thursday the Korean government reconfirmed that the Mountain Kumgang Tour may not be resumed without securing the definite guarantee on the personal safety of Korean tourists.

- **detain**: to prevent somebody from leaving or doing something; delay; keep somebody in an official place such as a police station
  (감금하다, 억류하다, 유치하다, 보류하다)

  예문 The police detained him as a suspect.
  (경찰은 그 사람을 용의자로 감금했다.)

- **alleged**: stated without being proved (멋대로 주장된, 추정된, 진위가 의심스러운)

  예문 She was detained for six days by North Korea for alleged spying during her tour of Mountain Kumgang.
  (금강산 관광도중 그녀는 스파이 혐의로 북한당국에 6일간 억류되었다.)

- **convince**: to cause somebody to believe that something is the case; persuade somebody to do something (~에게 납득시키다, 설득시키다)

  예문 How can I convince you of her honesty?
  (그녀가 정직하다는 것을 어떻게 말씀드리면 될까요?)

- **defect**: to leave a political party or country and go to another
  (도망하다, 탈주하다, 망명하다, 이탈하다)

  예문 She defected from the Liberals and joined the Socialists.
  (그녀는 노동당을 탈당하여 사회주의당원이 되었다.)

- **tug-boat**: a small powerful boat for pulling ships, especially into harbour (예인선)

  예문 She arrived at Sokcho port in the East Sea aboard a Hyundai's tug-boat.
  (그녀는 현대그룹의 예인선을 타고 동해 속초항에 도착했다.)

27

How To Open a Bottle of Champagne

Champagne should be drunk chilled; make sure the bottle is cold. This also

lessens the explosive effects of cork-popping.

1. Remove the aluminum foil wrapping over the cork.

2. Undo the safety wiring binding the cork to the bottle by grasping the little loop in the wire and turning in a counter-clockwise direction, until you can lift it off.

3. Holding the bottle firmly with one hand and the cork with the other - bottle pointed away from your face and others - turn the bottle (rather than the cork) slowly as you exert a slight upward pressure on the cork.

The cork should come out with nothing more than a polite sigh - the mark of the connoisseur. If it pops loudly and flies into the air, the bottle is probably too warm or has been agitated too much.

어휘

- **undo**: to reverse the doing of; do away with; unfasten by releasing; untie or loose (원상태로 돌리다, 제거하다, 지워 없애다, 취소하다, 파멸시키다)

  예문 He undid the gate. (그는 문을 열었다.)

  In the end their evil behaviour undid him.
  (결국 그들의 사악한 행동이 그를 파멸시켰다.)

- **safety wiring**: 철사로 된 안전 장치

  예문 He turned the safety wiring in the bottle. (그는 병의 안전 장치를 돌렸다.)

- **loop**: a curved or circular shape in something long; a piece of rope around an object (고리, 고리 모양의 손잡이, 고리처럼 둥근 것)

  예문 You can make a loop by a string. (줄로 고리를 만들 수 있다.)

- **counter-clockwise**: in the opposite direction to the direction in which the hands of a clock move; anticlockwise (시계 반대 방향으로)

  예문 They travelled in a counter-wise direction round the country.

(그들은 시계 반대 방향으로 그 나라를 여행했다.)

○ **exert**: to excercise ability or influence; put into vigorous action or effort
(힘을 쓰다, 행사하다, 영향을 미치다)

> **예문** She exerted every effort in this work. (그녀는 이 일에 모든 힘을 기울였다.)
> He exerted himself to improve the working condition.
> (그는 작업 환경을 개선하기 위해 전력을 다했다.)

○ **sigh**: a deep breath that is loud enough to be heard as a way of expressing
certain feelings such as sorrow, weariness or relief (한숨, 탄식)

> **예문** He breathed a deep sigh of relief at the news of releasing them.
> (그는 그들이 풀려났다는 소식을 듣고 안도의 한숨을 쉬었다.)
> With a sigh, she went out of her office.
> (한숨을 쉬면서 그녀는 사무실 밖으로 나갔다.)

○ **connoisseur**: a person who is especially competent to pass critical judgements
in art or in matters of taste; a discerning judge of the best in
any field (전문가, 권위자)

> **예문** She is a connoisseur of medieval art. (그는 중세 미술의 전문가이다.)
> He wants to be a connoisseur of jewels.
> (그는 보석 감정 전문가가 되고 싶어한다.)

○ **pop**: to make a short, quick and explosive sound; burst open with such a
sound; come or go quickly, suddenly or unexpectedly; protrude from the
socket (핑하는 소리를 내다, 핑하고 터지다, 불쑥 오다, 갑자기 나가다)

> **예문** The cork of the bottle popped in the air.
> (그 병의 코르크 마개가 핑 하는 소리를 내며 튀어나갔다.)
> He popped into the office with his son.
> (그는 아들을 데리고 사무실에 불쑥 나타났다.)

○ **agitate**: to move or force into violent, irregular action; shake or move briskly;
move to and pro (흔들다, 휘젓다, 뒤흔들다, 동요하게 하다, 선동하다)

> **예문** The strong wind agitates the sea.(강풍으로 바다가 거칠어지고 있다.)
> The riot agitated the public.(그 폭동으로 민심이 동요했다.)
> He became quite agitated when he was asked about his criminal past.
> (범죄 경력에 대한 질문을 받았을 때 그는 매우 흥분했다.)

28

**DON'T MISS THE IRRESISTIBLE
NEW LEGAL THRILLER
FROM JOHN GRISHAM
AMERICA'S #1
BESTSELLING AUTHOR**

Eleven-year-old Mark Sway has a deadly secret. The police want it. The federal prosecutor want it. The F.B.I. want it. And the Mob will kill him if he tells...

Available on March 3, 2009 at your local book store, or if you prefer, order direct from Doubleday. For information and credit card orders(VISA, MASTER card, American Express, Optima), call toll-free 1 (800) 223-6834 X9479.

THE CLIENT by John Grisham

Hardcover *0-385-42471-X *$23.50/$27.50 in Canada

어휘

○ **irresistible**: incapable of being resisted or withstand; lovable; tempting to possess
(억누를 수 없는, 저항할 수 없는, 압도적인, 매력적인, 아주 귀여운)

예문 I cannot overcome the irresistible desire for it.
(그것을 갖고 싶은 욕망을 억누를 수가 없다.)

○ **legal**: involving the law or the use of law (법적인, 법률의, 법정의)

예문 We should pay the legal fee. (우리는 법정수수료를 내야한다.)

○ **thriller**: a book, film or play that tells an exciting story about dangerous, frightening or mysterious events (추리 소설, 오싹하게 하는 것, 드릴러물)

예문 The movie is a thriller which makes us in suspense.
(그 영화는 우리 마음을 조마조마하게 하는 드릴러물이다.)

○ **deadly**: tending to cause death; fatal; like death; excessive; extremely accurate
(치명적인, 신랄한, 극단적인, 과도한, 견딜 수 없는)

예문 The air was deadly hot. (날씨가 너무나 더웠다.)

○ **federal**: consisting of a group of states controlled by a central government
(연방의, 연맹의, 연방제의, 연방정부의)

예문 In federal country, each state has its own local powers and laws.
(연방 국가에서는 주마다 독자적인 권한과 법이 있다.)

● **prosecutor**: a lawyer who tries to prove in a trial that the person who is on trial is guilty (검찰관, 검사, 기소자, 고발자)

예문 The special prosecutor is working on the case.
(특별 검사는 지금도 그 사건을 다루고 있다.)

● **mob**: a riotous crowd of people; a crowd engaged in lawless violence; a criminal gang; Mafia (폭도, 집단, 대중, 마피아: the Mob)

예문 The mob is led by emotions. (대중은 감정에 이끌린다.)

● **toll-free**: made, used or provided without a charge (무료의, 무료 장거리 전화의)

예문 You can use the toll-free phone number to order this book.
(무료 장거리 전화로 이 책을 주문할 수 있다.)
This is a toll-free highway. (여기는 무료 고속도로이다.)

29

NUMBERS

147million : The number of people worldwide connected to the Internet, almost half of them in the U.S.

$5.28billion : The estimated fortune of Liechtenstein's royal family, far more than Britain's Windsors, worth a mere $4.32billion.

27million : The estimated number of individuals around the world held in some form of slavery.

27.9% : The proportion of Russian women who are fat; only 6.3% of Italian women are similarly classified.

10billion : The number of marine viruses in a liter of seawater.

● **estimate**: to make an approximate calculation of an amount or quantity
(추정하다, 어림잡다, 짐작하다, 평가하다.)

예문 They estimated that he would go two hundred miles away after three hours. (그가 세 시간 후에는 200마일쯤 갈 것이라고 대략 추정했다.)

- **slavery**: the system by which people can be owned by other people; the state of not being free (노예의 처지, 노예 제도, 예속, 포로)

  예문 He has led the movement for the abolition of slavery.
  (그는 노예 제도 폐지 운동에 앞장서 왔다.)

- **proportion**: the amount or number of one kind of thing compared to the other things in the group (비율, 균형, 조화, 몫, 할당분)

  예문 The proportion of the unemployed workers are increasing this year.
  (올해 실직자의 비율이 점점 늘어가고 있다.)

30

Allergy

According to the National Institute of Allergy and Infectious Diseases, as many as 1 in 5 Americans has some form of allergy. About 50 percent of these people suffer from hay fever. Allergies rank sixth in the cost on the list of chronic diseases in the United States.

Pollen counts tend to be highest in the morning —especially between 5 and 10 a.m. The best time to exercise and do other outdoor activities is mid to late-afternoon when pollen counts tend to dip.

While people once believed that they were allergic to dust, researchers now know it is not the dust itself, but rather the mites that live in it that cause the problem. Between 100 and 500 individual mites live on a single gram of dust. Allergic reactions to pets are not determined by the breed of animal or the length of hair. The real problem is a protein in the skin and saliva of cats and dogs, not the hair.

어휘

- **hay fever**: an illness rather like a bad cold, but caused by pollen, dust from plants, which is breathed in from the air (여름철에 꽃가루로 인해 생

기는 코·목구멍 따위에 생기는 알레르기성 질환, 화분증, 건초열)

예문 Hay fever affects the person who has allergy to a pollen of a flower.
(건초열은 꽃가루에 알레르기 반응을 보이는 사람에게 나타난다.)

● **chronic**: lasting an illness for a very long time (만성의, 고질병을 가진, 만성적인)

예문 In spite of his chronic heart disease, he has helped other patients.
(그는 만성 심장 질환을 앓고 있음에도 불구하고 다른 환자들을 돌봐왔다.)

● **pollen** : a fine powder produced by flowers (꽃가루, 화분)

예문 A pollen is a cause of an allergy to some people.
(꽃가루에 알레르기 반응을 일으키는 사람들도 있다.)

● **dip**: to make a downward movement (내려가다, 가라앉다, 아래로 기울다)

예문 The birds dipped and flew over the house.
(새들은 아래로 날아 내려와 지붕 위로 날아갔다.)

● **mite**: a very tiny creature living in the skin or fur of animals (진드기)

예문 There are many kinds of mite in the plants and animals.
(식물과 동물의 몸에는 여러 종류의 진드기균이 살고 있다.)

● **saliva**: the watery liquid that forms in your mouth; spittle (타액, 침)

예문 Saliva helps you to digest food. (침은 소화를 돕는다.)

PART 2

• • •

핵심 문법

동사와 시제

A. 문장의 기본 형식과 구성 요소(주어, 동사, 목적어, 보어)

1. 주어(Subject) : 문장의 주체이며, 동사가 나타내는 행위나 상태의 주체가 되는 말

    _____ + 동사 + 보어. 목적어 + 문장수식어

    명사/대명사/명사구/부정사/동명사/명사절(that절, what절, wh-의문사절)

2. 동사(Verb) : 주어의 동작이나 상태를 나타내는 말

    ① 문장에 있어서 능동태와 수동태를 구분해야 한다.

    All animals connect in the great circle of life. (→ are connected)

    ② 본 동사를 찾자.

    The city Seoul covering over 100 square miles. (→ covers)

    The city Seoul to cover over 100 square miles. (→ covers)

    ③ 주어와 동사가 일치해야 한다.

    Economics are not in fact one of practical subjects for managers. (→ is)

    ④ 시제가 일치해야 한다.

    Parker was a sincere man who answers his mail every day.(→ answered)

3. 목적어(Object) : 동사 행위의 대상이 되는 말로서 (~을/를)로 해석되는 것을 말한다.

    명사/ 대명사/명사구/부정사/동명사/명사절(that절, what절, wh-의문사절)이 목적어 자리에 올 수 있다.

4. 보어(Complement) : 주어나 목적어를 보충해 주는 말로 주어가 될 수 있는 **명사** 상당어구와 **형용사**가 보어가 될 수 있다.

1. The number of the students who applied for the visas _____ quite great.

    a) are   b) was

    c) had   d) have been

2. Daily newspapers _____ people in touch with the world.

    a) keeping   b) to keep

    c) keeps   d) keep

3. The C.E.O. needs_____ the staffs of his retirement.

    a) to inform   b) inform

    c) informing   d) information

4. The committee has review the new equipment for 3 weeks at the production
                     a)   b)   c)   d)

line in the factory.

5. The Civic Theater _____ the half of money from one movie to be shown

to the public.

    a) donate   b) donation

    c) donates   d) was donated

6. He had barely _____ filming the habitat of the skylarks.

    a) finish   b) to finish

    c) finished   d) finishing

7. Close supervisor is necessary to prevent possible cheating during the mid-
            a)   b)   c)   d)

term exams.

8. The new managing director will _____ to the employees on the new agenda.

    a) tell   b) say

    c) speak   d) discuss

1. b)   2. d)   3. a)   4. a)   5. c)   6. c)   7. a)   8. c)   정답

1. She talked _____ her health problem with a doctor.

    a) to   b) about

    c) with   d) on

2. They say <u>that</u> there <u>are</u> sharp downturn <u>at</u> the stock market <u>this year</u>.
                 a)   b)   c)   d)

3. <u>Despite</u> his poor <u>appearance</u> he <u>looked like</u> sharp <u>in</u> the blue suit.
    a)   b)   c)   d)

4. Even a much experienced speaker gets _____ when asked to deliver a speech before a multitude of crowd.

    a) nervousness   b) nervous

    c) nervously   d) being nervousness

5. Feel free to take advantage of fully equipped child care center _____ to all members at no extra cost.

    a) affordable   b) capable

    c) available   d) agreeable

6. Many of the applicants who submitted their resume were _____ for the position.

    a) capable   b) eligible

    c) able   d) right

7. Due to the spirited competition among the contestants the decision on the winner was not _____ to make.

   a) eager
                 b) easy

   c) right
                 d) good

8. When recruits are well educated for the new gadget, many accidents can be _____.

   a) protected
           b) prevented

   c) solved
              d) reported

9. She tried to attend _____ the seminar, but she couldn't afford the time to do.

   a) on
                 b) to

   c) for
                d) at

10. They called _____ the meeting which was impossible to join.

   a) up
                 b) in

   c) for
                d) off

11. The supervisor suggested _____ that the construction should begin on schedule.

   a) me
                 b) to me

   c) at me
             d) for me

12. The doctor <u>said me</u> that <u>I must</u> stop <u>drinking</u> <u>to improve</u> my health.
                  a)   b)   c)   d)

13. The personnel department _____ expenses more than expected.

   a) has bought
         b) has spent

   c) has tried
           d) has used

14. The Magic department store has a big post-holiday _____ on remaining inventory.

   a) sale
                 b) sell

   c) sold
                d) selling

15. The marketing team wants to _____ the reaction of the consumers.

   a) gear   b) gauge

   c) grip   d) guard

16. This note will offer you _____ for the next meeting.

   a) remember   b) remembrance

   c) reminder   d) remembered

17. That new person from the branch office <u>who</u> <u>is</u> <u>working</u> with us reminds me <u>to</u>
                                          a) b) c)   d)

my uncle.

18. If you know the benefits of this formal contract, please explain

   _____.

   a) them to me   b) me them

   c) to me them   d) me as them

19. She _____ her marriage to her friends as soon as she saw them.

   a) arranged   b) announced

   c) assured   d) argued

20. The burglar _____ him of what he has.

   a) stole   b) robbed

   d) introduced   d) supplied

C. 시제

1. 단순시제

   a) 현재

   Mr. White has a large farm of three hundred acres.

   Tom gets up at six in the morning.

   The earth moves round the sun once a year.

   Tom starts (=will start) for London tomorrow morning.

   We will go on a picnic if it is fine tomorrow.

   Now Caesar crosses the Rubicon and enters Italy with 5,000men.

   * 시간, 조건의 부사절 : 시간(when, before 등), 조건(if, unless)의
     미래 부사절은 미래 시제 대신 현재 시제를 쓴다.

     I don't know if it will be fine tomorrow.

     Tell me the time when he will come.

   b) 과거

   Tom was a teacher when he was young.

   Ted usually got up at six in those days.

   Judy never heard (=I have never heard) of such a thing.

   After Tom finished (=had finished) his homework, he began to
   read the novel.

   c) 미래

   * will의 특별 용법

     ⓐ Tom will often come here on Sundays.

     ⓑ Dogs will bark when strangers come near them.

     ⓒ Judy will have her own way in everything.

     ⓓ The horse will not drink water. (=refuses to)

   * shall의 특별 용법

     ⓐ The Republic of Korea shall be a democratic.

     ⓑ Ask, and it shall be given you.

2. 완료시제

   a) 현재 완료 : 현재 완료(have+p.p.)는 어떤 동작 상태가 과거에서 현재까지 「완료, 경험, 결과, 계속」을 나타낸다.

     I have just finished my homework.

     I have never heard him speak ill of others.

     Mary has lost her eyesight.

     (=She lost her eyesight, and so she can't see now.)

     Tom has been ill since last Sunday.

     Ted has been studying English for five years.

     I will go to the movies when I have finished this task.

     • 미래 완료의 대용 : 시간, 조건의 부사절에서는 미래 완료 대신에 현재 완료를 쓴다.

     • 명확한 과거를 나타내는 부사(구) yesterday, last week, ago, just now 등과 의문 부사 When절은 현재 완료 시제로 못 쓰고 과거 시제로 쓴다.

     He has started just now.(×)→He started just now.(○)

     When have you finished it?(×)→When did you finish it?(○)

   b) 과거 완료

     I gave him the watch that I had bought in Switzerland.

     I had just finished my homework when he came.

     I recognized him at once, for I had seen him several times before.

     I remembered that I had lost my expensive watch.

     Mary had been ill for two weeks, when she was sent to hospital.

     I had been reading for two hours when he came to see me.

   c) 미래 완료

     I shall have finished this work by tomorrow.

     If I climb the mountain once more, I shall have climbed it three times.

     Mary will have bought a new house when his son leaves school.

     Ted will have been ill for two weeks by tomorrow.

3. 진행시제

    a) 단순 진행

        Ted is writing a letter to his friend in Busan.

        Mary is always complaining her husband.

        They are leaving (=will leave) Seoul tomorrow.

        Tom was playing baseball when I called on him.

        It will be snowing when you get to Seoul.

    b) 완료 진행형

        Judy has been playing the piano since this morning.

        Mary had been reading the novel for one hour, when he came.

        Tom will have been working here for five years by April.

      • 진행형을 쓰지 못하는 동사

        ① 「상태, 소유」: be, resemble, exist, seem, belong, have, possess 등

        ② 「감정, 심리 상태」: like, hate, fear, remember, respect, think, wish 등

        ③ 「지각, 인식」: see, hear, feel, smell, taste, understand, believe 등

    단, 원래의 뜻이 바뀌어 동작의 뜻을 갖거나 일시적 동작이나 상태를 강조할 때는 진행형을 쓸 수 있다.

    Tom is hearing his lecture. (hear=listen to)

    We are having supper now. (have=eat)

1. <u>On</u> weekdays, the library <u>opened</u> at 9:00 a. m. and closes <u>at</u> midnight.
   a)   b)   c)   d)

2. If you <u>will have</u> any <u>suggestions</u> <u>concerning</u> today's meeting, please give
          a)   b)   c)

me a <u>call</u> at anytime.
    d)

3. He _____ he was going to need a modem to access the computer information network.

   a) knows   b) knew

   c) will know   d) has known

4. <u>As soon as</u> I <u>will graduate</u>, I am <u>going to</u> return <u>to</u> my hometown.
        a)   b)   c)   d)

5. The copy machine will not be <u>fixed</u> <u>until</u> the repairman <u>will return</u> with the
                                 a)   b)   c)

special <u>tools</u> he has to go get.
         d)

6. We <u>took</u> him to the hospital <u>last Wednesday,</u> and <u>had been</u> there to see him
    a)   b)   c)

twice <u>since then</u>.
        d)

7. When the members <u>will be</u> <u>unable</u> to attend the conference they <u>should</u> see
                    a)   b)   c)

John Hansen <u>for</u> the next session.
           d)

8. The engineers insist that the new gadget _____ redesigned.

   a) is   b) should

   c) be   d) will be

D. 조동사(Auxiliary)

1. may

   may have P.P ~였는지도 모른다. **She may have been** hurt.

   (=Perhaps she was hurt.)

   might have P.P ~였었는지도 모른다. She **might have been** hurt.(=Perhaps she had been   hurt.)

   You **may well** be proud of your grade. (~하는 게 당연하다.)

   You **may as well** go at once. (~하는 게 낫다)

   You **might as well** take a rest. (~하는 게 낫다)-might는 공손함을 나타낸다.

2. can

   cannot be ~일리가 없다. The story **cannot be** true.

   cannot have p.p ~였을리가 없다. He **cannot have said** so.

3. must

   must be (~임에 분명하다) He **must be** thirty. It **must be** true love.

   must have p.p (~였음에 분명하다.) She must have lost her way.

4. should

   should have+P.P. You should have come earlier for the important gathering.

   〈조동사 + have+P.P〉

   1. cannot have P.P ~였을 리가 없다 (과거의 강한 추측) He **cannot have gone** far yet.

   2. could have P.P. ~할 수도 있었을 텐데 I **could have come** yesterday, but I did not want to.

   3. may have P.P. ~였을지 모른다.(과거의 추측) He **may have gone** home before we arrive there.

   4. must have P.P. ~였음에 틀림없다.(과거의 당연한 추측) I must have made a mistake.

   5. should have P.P. ~했어야 했는데(실현못한 과거 일에 대한 후회) You should have listened to his advice.

6. ought to have P.P. (= should have p.p) You **ought to have reported**
the suspect to the police.

7. need not have P.P. ~할 필요가 없었는데 You **need not have done** it
after all.

8. had better have P.P. ~하는 편이 나았었는데 She **had better have left**
London.

9. would rather have P.P. ~하느니 차라리 ~하겠다.

   I would rather have died than taken the loathsome task.

1. You _____ accept the transfer as soon as it was offered.
   a) cannot   b) ought
   c) would   d) had better

2. They <u>thought</u> the car accident must <u>have causing</u> severe <u>casualties</u> <u>on</u> a
       a)   b)   c)   d)
foggy night.

3. Photocopiers are <u>used to</u> <u>make</u> copies of a <u>written</u> text or <u>duplicating</u> any parts
                   a)   b)   c)   d)
in books.

4. Jason absents himself from the class, he _____ be sick in today.
   a) should   b) must
   c) will   d) would rather

5. The internet guide is _____ to be a very useful book.
   a) analyzed   b) supposed
   c) accorded   d) gathered

6. I thought my car insurance <u>would</u> cover all the <u>damages</u>, but the insurance
                                a)   b)
company must have <u>interpreting</u> the policy <u>in a</u> different way.
                       c)   d)

7. Her husband is <u>usually</u> supposed <u>to coming</u> home early <u>without fail</u>.
          a)   b)   c)   d)

8. You <u>had</u> better not <u>deal the</u> damage <u>caused</u> by the traffic accident <u>for</u> your
          a)   b)   c)   d)

own good.

1. d) 2. b) 3. d) 4. b) 5. b) 6. c) 7. c) 8. b) **정답**

E. 일치

▪ 주어와 술어 동사의 일치

  1. (a) The doctor and novelist is present at the meeting.

     (b) Bread and butter is his usual breakfast.

     (c) Slow and steady wins the race.

     (d) Every boy and (every) girl was delighted.

  2. (a) Twelve years is a long time to live abroad.

     (b) Mathematics is my favorite subject.

  3. (a) My family is a large one.

     (b) My family are all healthy.

  4. (a) Either he or I am in the wrong.

     (b) I as well as he have passed the examination.

     (c) The number of the students in our class is fifty.

        A number of the students in our class are absent.

     (d) Three-fourths of the earth's surface is water.

        Three-fourths of my friends have passed the examination.

▪ 시제의 일치

  1. He often tells me how he does (or, did, will do) it.

  2. (a) I think that he is ill.→I thought that he was ill.

(b) I think that he has been ill.→I thought that he had been ill.

(c) I think that he was ill.→I thought that he had been ill.

(d) I think that he will come.→I thought that he would come.

※ 시제 일치의 예외

① Our teacher said that the earth goes round the sun.(진리)

② I told him that I take a walk every morning.(현재의 사실, 습관)

③ We learned that Columbus discovered America in 1492.(역사적 사실)

④ I think that he could do it if he had more capital.(가정법)

→ I thought that he could do it if he had more capital.

⑤ It was colder yesterday than it is today.(비교의 부사절)

1. Speaking English fluently needs time, effort, and _____ to it.

  a) enthusiastic　　　　　　　　　b) enthusiast
  c) enthusiasm　　　　　　　　　　d) enthusiastically

2. Neither the sales nor the profit are expected to increase in the near future.
  a)　　　　　　　　　　　　b)　　　　　c)　　　　　　d)

3. The barber's and the dentist's lies between 5th and Main.
  　　　　　　　　a)　　　b)　　　　　　c)　d)

4. The clients seems to have no problem at all, even after the supplier increased
  a)　　　　　　　　　　　　b)　　　c)　　　d)

  prices.

5. After a long break from the sport he as well as his brother have made a
  a)　　　　　　　　　　　　　　　　　　　　　　　b)

  comeback and shocked the world of professional boxing.
  　　　　　　c)　　　　　　　　d)

6. Until the beginning of this year, the Gallery _____ not popular enough to visitors.

   a) is   b) was

   c) has   d) being

7. The company <u>along with</u> other companies <u>are</u> lowering the price of the products
                a)   b)

<u>in response to</u> the consumers' <u>demands</u>.
     c)   d)

8. Holly's <u>efficient</u> and enthusiasm are to be <u>praised</u>, and his colleagues <u>wish</u>
          a)   b)   c)

him the <u>best</u> in his new job.
        d)

9. Since direct flights <u>is</u> well <u>reserved</u>, you don't have to worry <u>about</u> your
                a)   b)   c)

<u>departure</u>.
   d)

10. <u>All</u> the people <u>who</u> attended the <u>conference</u> <u>needs to</u> report to their
   a)   (b)   c)   d)

supervisors later.

부정사(Infinitive)

Chapter 2

A. 정시·용법

■ 부정사의 명사기능

　1. to부정사는 명사처럼 주어/목적어/보어/동격이 될 수 있음.

　　To share the newspaper on the subway is indecent manners.

　　Preschoolers usually hope to go to school as soon as possible.

　　His dream was to be a fund manger, not an entrepreneur.

　　His desire, to be a fund manger, will be come true someday.

　2. 의문사 + to부정사: 명사적용법임.

　　Can you show me how to use the copier

■ 부정사의 형용사기능

　1. 명사+ to부정사 패턴임.

　　I have no friend to have a heart-to-heart talk.

　2. be+ to부정사 예정. 의무. 가능. 운명. 소망(예의가없어 연상).

　　The greenhouse is to be constructed by November.

■ 부정사의 부사기능

　목적/원인/결과/조건/이유판단의 근거/정도/독립부정사

　Workers work hard not to be laid off during recession.

　The woman is distributing the papers to hold the meeting.(목적)

　I'm glad to see you, tonight.(원인)

　She was so beautiful to take my breath away.

　= She was so beautiful that she took my breath away.(결과)

To hear him speak English, you would take him for a nigger. (조건)

My boss must be warm-hearted

to make regular donations to charity.(근거)

Muffins in this basket are not good to eat.(정도)

To tell the truth, she was a janitor, not a staff member.(독립부정사)

---

1. The Asian economy is predicted _____ by the turn of the year.

a) not to improve   b) improving

c) improve   d) not improved

2. All of the members are expected _____ their holidays during the summer season.

a) take   b) taking

c) to take   d) took

3. He managed _____ the goods by himself.

a) to finish to pack   b) to finishing packing

c) to finish packing   d) for finishing packing

4. Tell him _____ lose those parcels in any case.

a) don't   b) not

c) to not   d) not to

5. Various systems have been created to help executives _____ their time better.

a) manage   b) managing

c) manager   d) management

6. <u>Even</u> the summer months, <u>almost all</u> surfers wear wet suits to allow them
  a)   b)

<u>staying</u> in the water for long periods <u>without</u> becoming too cold.
  c)   d)

7. The brand new equipment is <u>to be operated</u> to maximize the <u>effective</u> of the
a)   b)

  generator which <u>is</u> essential <u>for</u> the equipment.
            c)   d)

8. The new <u>marketing</u> team had <u>begun launched</u> the new <u>type of</u> ice cream
         a)   b)   c)

  <u>targeting</u> younger generation.
     d)

9. You need _____ any receipts while you do shopping

  a) receive   b) to receive

  c) receiving   d) reception

10. The <u>inspectors</u> are <u>at odds</u> <u>to finding</u> the critical clues in the <u>murder</u> case.
         a)   b)   c)   d)

11. He decided to <u>moving</u> to a new apartment, <u>since</u> his neighbors continued
               a)   b)

  <u>making</u> much <u>noise</u>.
     c)   d)

12. The customers <u>wanted</u> the author to <u>autographed</u> many <u>copies</u> of his work
              a)   b)   c)

  which they <u>bought</u>.
          d)

13. <u>In order to</u> <u>equalizer</u> the nation's <u>trade imbalance</u>, we must increase exports
   a)   b)   c)

  or <u>reduce imports</u>.
         d)

14. Market <u>analysts</u> found <u>it</u> difficult <u>accounting</u> the sudden surge <u>in</u> market demand.
           a)   b)   c)   d)

15. Every drivers who wants to rent a car should know that rental cars are supposed to be _____ on time.

a) retired   b) returned

c) remade   d) remodeled

1. a) 2. c) 3. c) 4. d) 5. a) 6. c) 7. b) 8. b) 9. b) 10. c)
11. a) 12. b) 13. b) 14. c) 15. b)

정답

B. 주의해야 할 부정사

■ 독립부정사

to tell the truth, so to speak, strange to say, to be frank with you, to conclude, to say the least(of it), to be sure, to do one justice, to begin with, to make the story short

■ 부정사의 의미상 주어

It is wrong to tell a lie. (=It is wrong that we should tell a lie.)

I expect to succeed. (=I expect that I shall succeed.)

I expect you to succeed. (=I expect that you will succeed.)

It is difficult for me to solve this problem.

It is very kind of you to help us.

■ 부정사의 시제 : 단순형과 완료형

(a) He seems to be ill. (=He seems that he is ill.)

(b) He seemed to be ill. (=He seemed that he was ill.)

(a) He seems to have been a great scholar.

   =It seems that he was (of, has been) a great scholar.

(b) He seemed to have been a great scholar.

   =It seemed that he had been a great scholar.

(a) I expect him to succeed.(=I expect that he will succeed.)

(b) I expected him to succeed.(=I expected that he would succeed.)

   I intended to have seen her.(=I had intended to see her.)

   = I intended to see her, but I couldn't.

- **과거에 실현하지 못한 사실**

  (소망, 계획 동사의)과거 + to + have + p.p.(완료 부정사)

  =(소망, 계획 동사의) 과거완료 + to + 동사 원형(단순부정사)

- **원형 부정사**

  We should be kind to others.(조동사)

  I saw him enter the room. (지각동사)

  Tom made me stand there. (사역동사)

  You had better give it up.(관용표현)

- **관용적 용법**

  had better (of, best) + 원형 부정사~ : 「~하는 편이 좋다(가장 좋다)」

  can't but + 원형 부정사~ : 「~하지 않을 수 없다」

  would rather(=sooner) + 원형 부정사 ~(than…): 「(…하느니 보다는)차라리 ~하겠다」

  do nothing but + 원형 부정사~ : 「오직 ~만 하다」

- **지각 동사, 사역 동사가 「수동태」로 되면 to-부정사가 온다.**

  Tom was seen to enter the room by me.

  I was made to stand there by him.

동명사(Gerund)

A. 정의·용법

■ 동명사

동사가 명사처럼 쓰이므로 주어, 목적어, 보어, 동격의 역할을 함. 전치사 뒤에 나오는 것도 동명사!

1. Arresting the criminal was not easy job at all.(주어)

2. I remember seeing her before. (목적어)

3. She has her own taste, driving alone at dawn. (동격)

4. Her dream was being a sit-com comedian.(보어)

5. She has gone without saying a word.(전+동명사)

---

1. He's always object to my not _____ the party's line.

    a) follow   b) following

    c) have followed   d) being followed

2. If you are looking for a job, it is _____ checking the classified ads in the papers.

    a) worth   b) valuable

    c) expensive   d) necessary

3. _____ one's work properly may be worse than not doing at all.

    a) Not do   b) Not to do

    c) Not doing   d) To do

4. There was no _____ how many people would come to the seminar.

   a) tell   b) to tell

   c) telling   d) have told

5. The henpecked husband was _____ wake his wife early in the morning.

   a) afraid of   b) afraid to

   c) afraid   d) afraid that

6. Arrivals of the planes are subject to _____ in case of foggy weather.

   a) be delayed   b) being delayed

   c) delayed   d) being delay

7. The cost of <u>renting</u> drilling equipment for <u>the rest</u> of the summer <u>would</u> be
              a)   b)   c)

<u>comparable of</u> buying used machinery.
      d)

8. They <u>would like to</u> receive <u>some information</u> on <u>to attend</u> the seminar which
               a)   b)   c)

will be <u>held</u> in New York.
      d)

B. 동명사의 관용적 용법

1. **There is** no know**ing** when something will come up.
2. **It is no good** [use] monitor**ing** prices, due to rising oil cost.
3. We **cannot help** hir**ing** a temp to fill in while our assistant manager is on his summer leave.
4. **It goes without** say**ing** that taking leave is essential for workers.
5. I don't **feel like** go**ing** to the movies tonight.
6. She **came near** be**ing** hit by a sedan.
7. He is busy (in) prepar**ing** for the final.
8. She doesn't **spend** much **time** (in) prepar**ing** for food.
   c.f) He spent all his money to buy a brand-new car. The car costed him an arm and a leg.
9. I **had difficulty** [a hard time] (in) tell**ing** a lie that my boss is out of town.

---

1. There is no _____ what will come up tomorrow, for such is a life.
   a) telling
   b) to tell
   c) for telling
   d) tell

2. He stayed <u>home</u> <u>alone</u>, <u>as</u> he was busy <u>to prepare</u> for his mid— term paper.
          a)   b)   c)   d)

3. The inspectors all had difficulty _____ the critical clues for the murder case.
   a) in to find
   b) finding
   c) to find
   d) find

4. The <u>principal</u> had to <u>suspend</u> the children from school, <u>since</u> they would not
          a)   b)   c)

   stop <u>to fight</u> in the classroom.
          d)

5. We had a very hard time _____ some of the questions

a) to discuss   b) discuss

c) of discussing   d) discussing

6. They care about _____ prices from the government due to the rising cost of living.

a) monitoring   b) monitor

c) monition   d) monitory

7. The construction company failed <u>completing</u> finishing touches <u>on</u> the new
                                           a)   b)

apartment <u>within</u> the <u>planned</u> period of construction.
                 c)   d)

8. The cafe created elegant effect by_____ the table with hand- woven
cloth.

a) throwing   b) posing

c) spacing   d) draping

분사(Participle)

A. 정의·용법

■ 분사

1. 동사기능 : 시제, 수동형이 있으며, 보어, 목적어를 동반함.

   They sat waiting to be seated at the restaurant.

2. 형용사기능

   a. 한정용법 : 명사를 수식함.

      He comes from a broken home.

      He was a broken man after his business went broke.

   b. 서술기능 : 접속사+ 주어동사의 일부역할을 함.

      They were on a plane flying from New York to L.A.

      (c.f. I always fly business class. I'm flying to New York tomorrow.)

      Because the driver had been slightly wounded, the emergency crew walked him to the hospital.

      → The driver slightly wounded, the emergency crew walked him to the hospital.

1. <u>A</u> well- planned resume is <u>the first</u> step toward <u>finding</u> a <u>satisfied</u> job.
      a)   b)   c)   d)

2. <u>After signing</u>, the invoice was <u>handed over</u> to the <u>agent</u> as soon as <u>possible</u>.
       a)   b)   c)   d)

3. English is _____ as an international language all over the world.

   a) speaking   b) spoken

   c) spoke   d) speak

4. All things _____, you are still to blame.

   a) that we consider   b) considering

   c) considered   d) to consider

5. Anybody _____ the man in the photo is asked to call the police.

   a) knows   b) calls

   c) recognizing   d) a friend of

6. The manager is waiting for the new equipment was ordered yesterday.
                     a)   b)   c)   d)

7. Due to the _____ capacity, The mode will be replaced by any one better
to meet the versatile public.

   a) limit   b) limited

   c) limiting   d) limitation

8. According to the recent survey, there is a shortage of skilling people in the field
     a)   b)   c)   d)
of information technology.

9. They are very _____ in initiating the new project.

   a) interesting   b) interested

   c) interest   d) interests

10. The investigator studies the issues _____ in the murder case.

   a) involving   b) involved

   c) involves   d) involvement

1. d) 2. a) 3. b) 4. c) 5. a) 6. d) 7. b) 8. c) 9. b) 10. b) 정답

B. 분사 구조

1. 현재분사 : 능동, 진행의 의미.

    A rolling stone gathers no moss.

    ☞ A stone (which is) rolling gathers no moss.

2. 과거분사 : 수동, 완료의 의미.

    The cleaning crew was busy sweeping the fallen leaves on the back yard.

    ☞ The cleaning crew was busy sweeping the leaves which were fallen on the back yard.

    c.f.) Arresting the criminal Shin, the elusive, was not easy job at all. I regret having said so.

    She went without saying a word.

3. 분사구문

a. 주절의 주어와 일치하면 : 분사구문의 주어생략

    Though she lives next door, she never says hello to me.

    ☞ Living next door, she never says hello to me.

b. 주절의 주어가 다른 경우 : 주어를 살려주세요!

    As it was a beautiful day, we went hiking.

    ☞ It being a beautiful day, we went hiking.

    * hiking trails 등산로

c. 의미를 강조하려면 : 접속사를 살려주세요!(when, while, after, though의 경우)

    While I was walking up the street, I met Mr. Handsome.

    ☞ While(being)walking up the street, I met Mr. Handsome.

d. being 혹은 having been은 생략가능

    As he had been wounded in the leg, he couldn't walk.

    ☞ (Having been) Wounded in the leg, he couldn't walk.

---

1. _____ a fine day, we went on a hike through the forest.

   a) Having been   b) It being

   c) Being   d) It was

2. <u>Realize</u> she <u>had made</u> a <u>mistake</u>, she <u>repeated</u> the experiment.
    a)   b)   c)   d)

3. <u>Other things</u> <u>be</u> equal, the touch tone phone <u>is</u> <u>superior</u> to the rotary phone.
    a)   b)   c)   d)

4. After_____ his secretary to hold his calls, he was able to focus his attention on the meeting.
    a) to ask   b) asking
    c) being asked   d) to asking

5. It <u>goes</u> <u>without to</u> say that <u>nothing</u> is more important <u>than</u> good health.
    a)   b)   c)   d)

6. After <u>review</u> all the applications, the manager <u>chose</u> only one person <u>among</u>
        a)   b)   c)
much qualified <u>applicants</u>.
                d)

7. The host prepared various kinds of food for the disabled, _____ them to make themselves at home.
    a) to allow   b) allowance
    c) allow   d) allowing

8. The _____ plan of rebuilding is proceeding well.
    a) proposal   b) proposing
    c) proposed   d) proposes

1. b) 2. a) 3. b) 4. b) 5. b) 6. a) 7. d) 8. c) 정답

태(Voice)와 법(Mood)

A. 수동태에서 주의사항

1. "자동사 + 전치사(구) = 타동사구"로 생각하여 수동태를 만듦.

He laughed at me during the blind date. → **I was laughed at** by him during the blind date.

The Friday secretary took care of calling off the meeting.

→ Calling off the meeting **was taken care of** by the Friday secretary.

2. 행위자는 "y + 목적어" 씀.

We were supposed to attend the annual seminar, but rejected by the janitors.

- by 이외에 다른 전치사가 오기도 함.

He said that nothing would **be held at** the university, but a flea market was opened around the campus.

The fancy restaurant **was built in** 1965 when the present owner was not born.

- by 이외의 전치사 관용구

He's **known as** a writer.　　　　He's **known for** his book.

The book is **known to** everyone.　　The room **is filled with** computers.

He's **convinced of** his success.　　The story **is based on** the truth.

He **is associated with** the suspect.　He's **concerned with** the accident.

She **was surprised at** the news.

- make/let/have [get] + 목적어 + 과거분사
  (주어이외의 것, 즉 목적어를 수동으로 시킬 때)

He couldn't **make** himself **understood.**

Can you **let** yourself **relaxed?**

We **had** our tent **blown down** by the wind.

I **had** a letter **written** for me. I had you followed.

(누군가로 하여금 널 미행하도록 시켰거든)

• let/make/have + 목적어 + 동·원   get + 목적어 + to부정사

He **made** his secretary **take care of** the matter.

He got his secretary **to take care of** the matter.

Let me **know** the time when he comes back.

Please, **have** my customer **come** here at five.

1. When the proposal was <u>introduce</u>, <u>many of the</u> employees <u>expressed</u> doubts
                              a)   b)   c)

   <u>as to</u> its effectiveness.
     d)

2. Ten representatives <u>sent</u> <u>from</u> the home office to <u>attend</u> the <u>annual</u> conference.
                        a)   b)   c)   d)

3. The fact <u>that</u> he arrived at the office <u>late</u> was <u>known the manager</u> the <u>following</u>
              a)   b)   c)   d)

   day.

4. <u>According to</u> one of the union <u>officials</u>, the new labor contract <u>has accepted</u> by
        a)   b)   c)

   <u>all</u> the employees.
    d)

5. Customers should refer to the prices in the reply envelope _____ in

   the catalog.

   a) provide   b) provides

   c) provided   d) providing

6. Tourists visiting this historic site can enjoy _____ tours all the year round.

    a) guidance   b) guided

    c) guide   d) guiding

7. <u>According</u> to the recent survey, <u>there</u> is shortage of <u>skilling</u> people in the <u>field</u>
    a)   b)   c)   d)

of information technology.

8. After completing his role at the company, he _____ for his 20 years of service.

    a) honored   b) was honored

    c) praised   d) was reserved

1. a) 2. a) 3. c) 4. c) 5. c) 6. b) 7. c) 8. b)   정답

B. 법(Mood)

1. 법의 종류

문장의 내용에 대하여 말하는 사람의 심적인 태도를 나타내는 동사의 어형 변화를 「법」이라 하며 「직설법, 명령법, 가정법」의 3가지가 있다.

2. 명령법

1) Lend me your book, will you? (직접 명령)

2) (a) Let me know the time of your arrival. (간접 명령)

   (b) Let's go for a walk, shall we?

3) (a) Work hard, and you will succeed. (=If you work hard, you will~)
    (조건 명령)

   (b) Work hard, or you will fail. (=If you don't work hard, you will~)

4) (a) Go where you will (=Wherever you may go), you will be welcomed.
    (양보 명령)

ⓑ Try as you may, you can't please everybody.

   (=However hard you may try, you can't please everybody.)

ⓒ Be a man ever so rich, he should not be idle.

   (= However rich a man may be, he should not be idle.)

3. 가정법(subjunctive mood)

   1) 현재 : 현재나 미래의 불확실한 상황을 가정함.

      〈If + 주어 + 현재시제~, 주어 + will/shall/may/can/must〉

      If our company **goes** out of business, we **will** be out of work, too.

   2) 과거 : 현재사실에 대한 반대를 가정하므로 시점은 현재임.

      〈If + 주어 + 과거형동사 ~, 주어 + should/would/could + 동·원〉

      If he **had** enough money, he **would** buy a BMW.

      (= Because he doesn't have enough money, he can't buy a BMW)

      If I **were** you, Mr. Jason, I **wouldn't** be upset on the trivial matter.

   3) 과거완료

      〈If + 주어 + had + P.P~, 주어 + would/should/could/might + have + p.p〉

      If I had been you, I could not have ironed out the critical matter.

      주절의 "should have + p.p"는 과거에 대한 유감을 나타냄.

      You should have gone there.

      * if 절에는 "would/should+have + p.p"가 올 수 없다.

        If I would have been there, I could have helped her. (×)

   4) 가정법 미래 : 현재나 미래에 대해 가능성이 희박한 상황에서 가정함.

      〈If + 주어 + should~, 주어 + 조동사의 현재(will/shall등) / 조동사의 과거(would/should 등)〉

      〈If + 주어 + were to~, 주어 + 조동사의 과거(would/should/could/might)〉

      should는 가능성이 어느 정도 있음. were to는 불가능한 가정에 쓰임.

      If you should go to the cafe late in the evening, you could take the chance of taking a look at her.

      If the sun were to rise in the west, I would do it.

      (were to는 불가능한 가정)

1. If I _____ to Europe again, I will have been there four times.

    a) will go   b) go

    c) will have gone   d) will have been

2. If you don't have enough time to clean up, _____ it later.

    a) you could have done   b) you had done

    c) be doing   d) do

3. If she _____ the manager, she would not treat us so severely.

    a) were   b) are

    c) will be   d) would be

4. If I _____ English fluently, I would apply for the job.

    a) can speak   b) spoke

    c) will speak   d) speak

5. We could <u>have finished</u> the report <u>on time</u> if he <u>will have</u> given us <u>all</u> the
                  a)   b)   c)   d)

information in advance.

6. _____ today, he would get there by Friday.

    a) Would he leave   b) If he left

    c) If he will leave   d) If he had left

7. If I <u>would have had</u> more time, I would have <u>written</u> a <u>much</u> better and <u>far</u>
            a)   b)   c)   d)

more thorough report.

8. The farmers estimate that the crop yield <u>has doubled</u> <u>by the end of</u> the next
                                           a)   b)

year, <u>provided</u> the land is cultivated <u>according to</u> the schedule.
       c)   d)

4. 주의해야 할 가정법

1) **wish**

   I wish that I **met** you. (= I'm sorry that I can't meet you.)

   I wish that I **had gone** to the park. (= I'm sorry that I didn't go to the park.)

2) **unless** : unless이하에 부정어가 같이 쓰이지 않음.

   Unless you don't help me, I will not succeed in my life. (×)

   Unless you help me, I will not succeed in my life.(○)

3) **If의 생략**, 동사가 과거, 과거완료일 때 생략가능.

   Were I you(=If I were you) I would go there.

   Should you need (=If you should need) my help again, just give me a call.

   Had he come (=If he had come) sooner, he would have seen her.

4) **If 절의 생략** : 생략해도 알 수 있거나, 단어나 구의 일부에 if의 뜻이 포함이 될 때

   He **could** easily solve the problem.

   A true friend would tell you the truth.

   To hear him speak, you would think of him as a native speaker.

   I was ill, **otherwise**(= or) I would have come.

5) **If it were not for** your help, I couldn't succeed in my life.

   = **But for** your help, I couldn't succeed in my life.

   = **Without** your help, I couldn't succeed in my life.

---

1. If he had more time, he _____ go to the hospital to see her.

    a) would have   b) will

    c) would   d) has to

2. But for your timely advice, we could have been financially damage.
     a)   c)   c)   d)

3. If you <u>would have</u> <u>come</u> earlier you could have <u>filled</u> the <u>opening</u>.
          a)   b)   c)   d)

4. Complete what you have to do by tomorrow, _____ you won't be paid.
   a) otherwise   b) elsewhere
   c) unless   d) nevertheless

5. If you _____ me the chance, I would have explained my plans in more details.
   a) would have given   b) gave
   c) would give   d) had given

6. <u>Had</u> we known the road was <u>under</u> construction, we would <u>not take</u> the road
  a)   b)   c)
which was unable <u>to</u> access.
                  d)

7. Had Ms. Toth _____ , the city would have embarked on building of a new convention center.
   a) elected   b) been elected
   c) elect   d) election

8. <u>Should</u> you decide to <u>join into</u> the club <u>during</u> the next a few months, you will
  a)   b)   c)
<u>receive</u> 10% discount of any purchase.
  d)

명사(Noun), 대명사(Pronoun), 관계대명사(Relative Pronoun)

A. 명사(Noun)

1. 명사의 종류

• 고유명사: 특정지명, 인물, 특정대상. 장소 예) New York, KAL, Edison, Ford

  cf.) An Edison , A Ford, A Mr. Kim

• 추상명사: 인간의 생각속에 존재. 예) love, friendship, religion

• 집합명사: 여러 개인이 모여 형성된 것 예) family, police, class

  Almost every family in the country owns a Television set./All my family enjoy skiing./ Ten families live in this apartment.

  My class has over 1000 members. / My class are all TOEIC preparers.

• 보통명사 : 흔히 볼 수 있는 사물, 대상. 예) chair, student, school, orange

  cf) go to school/hospital

• 물질명사 : 눈으로 볼 수 없거나 일정 형태가 없어서 특정 단위를 씀. 예) water, coffee, glass, air a glass of water, a cup of coffee, a piece of glass, a breath of air

 cf) the waters(바다, 강, 호수) a glass (한 개의 유리잔, 유리제품, 거울)

   a pair of glasses(한벌의 안경), the air(대기, 하늘) an air of arrogance (거만한 태도)

2. 추상명사의 보통명사화

① 종류: Physics is **a science**

② 구체적 행위: They committed **a folly**.

③ 그러한 속성을 가진 사람: she's **a success/beauty/failure**

3. 절대복수(형태가 항상 복수임.)

① 병명 : measles, mumps, blues

② 학문 : ethics, politics, statistics, mathematics, phonetics

③ 고유명사 : Athens, the United States of America, the United Nations

④ 짝으로 된 명사 : gloves, pants, scissors, socks (복수취급) cf) a pair of pants (바지 한벌)

* 기타 news(뉴스) arms(무기)

---

1. The duty-free shop on the 3rd floor of the department store carries _____ of luxurious sports equipment.

   a) many   b) few

   c) much   d) not a few

2. <u>Economics</u>, with <u>their</u> widespread range of practical application, is of interest
    a)   b)

to business people in <u>the world</u>.
               d)

3. A squeaking sound is a good _____ of engine problems.

   a) show   b) indication

   c) specifications   d) sight

4. You must have your supervisor's _____ for leaving early from the office.

   a) approval   b) approve

   c) approves   d) to approve

5. The branch manager appreciated _____ he felt from the staffs in the main branch.

   a) wellness   b) hospitality

   c) benefit   d) altruism

6. Launching a <u>major</u> television <u>campaigner</u> is <u>to advertize</u> its <u>latest</u> soap opera.
　　　　　　　a)　　　　　　　　　　b)　　　　　　c)　　　　　　d)

7. Close <u>supervisor</u> is <u>necessary</u> to <u>prevent</u> possible <u>cheating</u> during the mid-term
　　　　　　a)　　　　　　　b)　　　　　c)　　　　　　　　d)

exams.

8. The personnel manager selected six _____ for the interviews.

　a) choices　　　　　　　　　　　　b) selection
　c) candidates　　　　　　　　　　d) narrow

B. 대명사(Pronoun)

■ it과 one의 용법

　it 〔they〕 : 특정명사를 대신하여 받음.(정관사, 소유격 동반명사)

　　　　　A : Do you have your wallet? B: Yes, I have it.(it= the wallet)

　one 〔ones〕 : 불특정명사(부정관사 동반명사)

　　　　　A : Do you have to buy a wallet B: Yes, I have to buy one.(=a
　　　　　　wallet)

• one/the other

　두개 중 한개가 one이면 나머지 하나는 the other

　I have two cats. One is white ; the other is black.

　* 셋이상의 경우에는 one, another, the other로 받음.

　　I have three balls. One of the three is red, another is yellow, and the
　　other is green

• others/ the others

　We should be kind to others (others: 다른 사람, 다른 것들)

　I have five cats. One is white; the others are black. (the others = the rest.
　특정 나머지 것들/사람들)

- Such의 주요용법

  1. Such A as B/ A such as B (B같은 A)

     Such birds as the lark and sparrow = birds such as the lark and sparrow

  2. 명사대신의 Such The minister wanted to be respected as such

     (such= the minister)

- Either/Neither의 용법

  1. 단수 취급함. Neither of your suggestions is enough to solve the problem.

  2. either(둘 중 어떤 것이라도) Either of your ties matches you well.

     neither(둘다 모두 …가 아니다) Neither of them goes to school.

  3. either A or B (A,B중 하나) / neither A nor B(A.B 둘다 ....가 아니다)

     * or, nor 다음 B에 수를 일치함.

     $$\begin{cases} \text{Either Tom or I am an Vriversity studert} \\ \text{Neither Tom nor I am an instructor} \end{cases}$$

- All

  All은 사물일 땐 단수/ 사람일 땐 복수

  All is lost (만사가 끝났다) All were happy.(다들 행복했다.)

  All of us were happy. (우리 모두는 행복했다.)

  c.f) All (of the) people, Most (of the) people, Many (of the) people

- Each/ Every 둘다 단수취급

  Each of us has his/her own bag. Each student has his/her own room.

  Every boy likes it. Every boy and girl knows the fact.

1. The girl thought the job was demanding too much of _____ time.

  a) its   b) her

  c) the   d) she's

2. Neither of <u>the applicants</u> <u>have</u> had experience <u>in</u> selling <u>sporting</u> goods.

                      a)   b)   c)   d

3. Each of them should <u>suggest</u> <u>their own</u> solution <u>to the problem</u> <u>at the meeting</u>.
                        a)   b)   c)   d)

4. Two brothers were both sick; _____ at school yesterday.
- a) either was
- b) either were
- c) neither was
- d) neither were

5. The project should be submitted to the marketing manager so that _____ can be approved.
- a) it
- b) its
- c) they
- d) their

6. Astonishgingly two candidates voted for each _____ at the mayor election.
- a) one
- b) other
- c) others
- d) ones

7. Because the shipment that was delivered was severly damaged, we are asking you send _____
- a) each other
- b) one another
- c) another
- d) other

8. <u>All</u> the people who attended the <u>conference</u> <u>needs</u> to <u>report to</u> their supervisors
   a)   b)   c)   d)

later.

C. 관계 대명사(Relative Pronoun)

▪ 관계대명사

관계라는 말속에 접속사가 있고 여기에 대명사를 붙임.

She loves her brother who is a lawyer.☞ She loves her brother, and he is a lawyer.

관계대명사절은 불완전한 문장이어야 한다.(주어, 목적어, 보어중 하나가 빠져있음.)

I know the city which he likes.(likes의 목적어가 없음) likes의 목적어는 which임.(여기안에 it이 포함됨.)

• 선행사에 따라

선행사 \ 격	주 격	소유격	목적격
사 람	who	whose	whom
사 물	which	of which, whose	which
사람, 사물, 사람+사물	that		that

• 관계사절에 주어가 없으면 주격, 목적어가 없으면 목적격임.

She is a foreigner who speaks English.(주격) She is the lady whom I saw the day before.(whom이 목적어)

She is the lady whose hand is beautiful. (whose hand가 주어의 역할)

▪ 관계대명사 that

① 관계대명사 who. which 대신 사용한다. The girl that lives opposite visited us. (=who)

② 선행사로 사람과 사물이 함께 올 때 사용한다. I saw the man and his horse that were crossing the street.

③ 선행사로 강한 한정어 'the + only/very/same/main/chief/서수/최상급 이 올 때 사용한다.

This is the only woman that I have loved in my life.

④ 선행사로 전부 혹은 全無(everything, all, both, no, nothing, little, none) 를 지칭하는 말이 올 때 사용된다.

His writings contains little that is new, but much that is old.

⑤ 전치사 뒤에 오지 못한다. This is the house in that I live.

   * that을 쓰지 않는 경우 : 앞에 comma가 있거나 전치사가 있을 때

   The boy, that is honest, is my son.(×) This is the place of that I spoke.(×)

■ 관계대명사 what

관계대명사 what= 선행사+ 관계대명사임.

What(=That which) is beautiful is not always good. I will do what(=all that) I can.

This is what(=the thing which) I want.

■ what을 응용한 관용구

A is to B what C is to D (A, B의 관계는 C,D의 관계와 같다.)

Reading is to the mind what food is to the body.

What with -- and (what with) ~ (--과 ~ 등으로)

What with overwork and what with hunger, he was ill.

What is + 비교급(더욱 --한 것은) / what is+ 최상급(가장 --한 것은)

What is better is that she is tender-hearted.

What is best is that she is smart.

■ 유사관계대명사 (As. But. Than)

접속사 as, but, than 중 쓰임이 관계대명사와 흡사한 것을 유사관계대명사라 한다.

① As : 선행사 속에 such, as, so, the same 등이 들어 있을 때 사용한다.

   She is such a lovely girl as everyone likes. (as가 likes의 목적어 구실을 함.)

   As many children as came were given some cake. (as가 came의 주어 구실을 함.)

② But : 선행사 속에 not, no, never, few, little등의 부정어가 들어 있을 때 사용하며 '---하지 않는' 의 뜻임.

   There is not a rule but has exception. (but이 has의 주어구실을 함.)

   There are few of us but wish to succeed.

③ Than : 선행사 속에 비교급이 들어 있을 때 사용한다.

   She has more money than you have. (than이 have의 목적어 구실을 함.)

   Don't use more words than are necessary. (than이 are의 주어구실을 함.)

1. Dalton was <u>the only one</u> of the guys <u>whom</u> as you know <u>was</u> not <u>qualified</u> for
                      a)   b)   c)   d)

the job.

2. She has no idea in <u>that</u> she will receive <u>from</u> her husband <u>for</u> her <u>twenty—fifth</u>
                         a)   b)   c)   d)

birthday.

3. Hawaii is one of the places _____ he wants to visit.

   a) which   b) where

   c) to where   d) in which

4. <u>We employees</u> went <u>to</u> Miami Beach <u>which</u> we found <u>many shells</u>.
      a)   b)   c)   d)

5. The retailor imported <u>many</u> suitcases <u>from</u> abroad, <u>that</u> are too expensive for
                           a)   b)   c)

the consumers <u>to</u> buy.
             d)

6. The building <u>which built</u> in 1948 is <u>demolished</u> <u>according to</u> the city plan of
               a)   b)   c)

rebuilding.
   d)

7. Many parents <u>during</u> the economic slowdown cannot <u>afford</u> the tuition fees that
              a)   b)

<u>they</u> <u>are</u> expensive enough.
  c)   d)

8. The project <u>which</u> they submitted early <u>in</u> the morning <u>has accepted</u> <u>by</u> the
             a)   b)   c)   d)

new president.

9. she didn't <u>want to</u> transfer to the department <u>what</u> was <u>notorious</u> for heavy
a)   b)   c)

<u>workload</u>.
   d)

10. Employment <u>benefits</u>, <u>that</u> are given <u>new</u> employees <u>have increased</u> greatly.
               a)   b)   c)   d)

11. It's a handy camera, and, _____ is better is that its price is very
reasonable.
  a) which   b) what
  c) as   d) that

12. She is not qualified for the job for _____ she applied.
  a) that   b) whom
  c) which   d) it

13. The applicant has been <u>waiting for</u> <u>the response was</u> not sent <u>for</u> three months
                          a)   b)   c)

from the <u>personnel department</u> of the company.
                  d)

14. The company must know _____ competitors are trying to accomplish.
  a) what   b) that
  c) whether   d) who

15. The only person <u>whose</u> name <u>is typing</u> <u>deserves</u> the service in the <u>fitness</u> club.
                      a)   b)   c)   d)

형용사(Adjective), 부사(Adverb), 관계부사(Relative Adverb)

A. 형용사(Adjective)

■ Many와 Much Few와 Little

1. many는 가산명사의 복수와 함께써서 사물이나 사람의 수가 많음을 나타냄. 복수취급함. much는 불가산명사로 쓰이며 양의 많음을 나타냄. many의 반대표현은 few이고 much의 반대표현은 little임.

   a. Many people die of cancer.

   b. He can speak many foreign languages.

   c. Many of us attended the meeting.

   d. Many at the meeting were very tired.

   * many a + 단수명사 → 단수동사 Many a school in the area is prestigious.

   * many와 바꿀 수 있는 표현[a good/great many, a great/large number of, a multitude of] + 복수명사

2. much는 불가산명사에 쓰이며 양의 많음을 나타낸다. 따라서 단수취급한다. (물질, 추상명사는 불가산 명사로 단수취급.)

   a. I don't drink much wine.

   b. You spend too much money.

   c. I have much to say about him.

   d. She doesn't think much about the matter.

   * much와 바꿔쓸 수 있는 표현[a good/great deal of]+물질명사/추상명사

   * a lot of/ lots of/(a) plenty of + 복수명사/물질명사, 추상명사

3. few "수가적어 거의 없는"의 뜻이며(부정) a few "수가 조금있는"의 뜻(긍정)이다.

a. Few artists live luxuriously.

b. A few people gathered there.

c. Many are called but few are chosen.

d. A few of them know the secret.

4. little "양이 거의 없는"의 뜻(부정)이며 a little "양이 조금있는"의 뜻(긍정)이다.

a. We have very little information.

b. We have a little information.

c. Little remains to be said.

d. He drank a little of water.

* not/no/quite a few → 상당히 많은(복수명사)

* not/quite a little, no little → 상당히 많은(물질명사/추상명사)

---

1. He seldom reads daily newspaper because he has _____ time.

a) a little   b) so little

c) few   d) much

2. The lawyer was not _____ that the witness was telling the truth.

a) convince   b) convinced

c) conviction   d) conveyed

3. _____ student carries dictionaries to look up the words unfamiliar with.

a) Many   b) Few

c) Little   d) Many a

4. Did you have _____ to do this afternoon?

a) much   b) many

c) any   d) so many

5. The research staffs in the lab are to know how to use the _____ equipment.

a) protect   b) protected

c) protective   d) protecting

6. If you turn to the right gift packing is _____ at a low cost.

    a) available   b) receivable

    c) probable   d) useful

7. <u>Learning</u> to play the piano is a <u>complexity</u> process, and <u>one</u> that require time
     a)   b)   c)

and <u>patience</u>.
        d)

8. The new benefits plan has <u>several of</u> additions, <u>including</u> summer <u>holidays</u>, and
                              a)   b)   c)

<u>flexible</u> work
   d)

9. The prime minister set aside _____ relief funds for the poor in the
town.

    a) addition   b) additional

    c) addicted   d) addict

10. The new brochure is very _____ when you read it carefully.

    a) indicative   b) informative

    c) interested   d) excited

1. b) 2. b) 3. d) 4. a) 5. c) 6. a) 7. b) 8. a) 9. b) 10. b)   정답

B. 비교(Comparatives)

■ 비교의 종류 : 원급비교, 비교급비교, 최상급 비교

Brad is as tall as Tom(원급 비교)

Brad is taller than Tom(비교급 비교)

Brad is the tallest guy in the schad

불규칙변화

good/well-better-best bad/ill-worse-worst many/much-more-most few-fewer
-fewest

late -later- latest(시간) He was later than I. This is the latest edition.

late- latter-last(순서) The story is in the latter part of the book. He was the
last for the meal

old-older-oldest(늙은)/old-elder-eldest(손위의)

1. 원급 비교 (*c.f 비교급/최상급수식 부사 even, much, by far, still, a lot)
   (1) as~as형 : 두 문장의 비교 내용이 같을 때 as(부사)~as(접속사)로 접속
      시킨다.

      She is 20 years old. + He is 20 years old. = She is as old as he (is old).
   (2) the same~as형 : 양측이 완전히 동일할 때, 앞의 **as** 대신 the same을
      쓴다.

      My dress is **the same** color as yours. This color is **the same as** that.
      This is **the same camera as** I lost. (동종물건) This is **the same camera
      that** I lost. (동일 물건)
   (3) 관용적 표현
      ① **as~as 주어 can = as~as possible** : 가능한 한 ~하게

         She will be back **as** soon **as she can**. I will get there **as** fast **as
         possible**.
      ② **as~as can be** : 더할 나위 없이, 그 이상 ~할 수 없게

         He is **as** poor **as can be**. I am **as** tired **as** can be.
      ③ **as good as** : ~한 거나 마찬가지다 She is **as good as** dead.
      ④ **as far[long] as** : ~하는 한 **As far[long] as** I am concerned, I agree
         with you.

1. We <u>never thought</u> <u>that</u> she could be as <u>friendlier</u> as she <u>is</u> today.
       a)   b)   c)   d)

2. The sun sets _____ in summer than in winter.
   a) latter   b) most late
   c) rapidly   d) later

3. The new stadium cannot accomodate _____ people as the old one.
   a) as good   b) so many
   c) so much   d) as much

4. Tell me_____information on the project which is urgent.
   a) many   b) little
   c) more   d) a few

5. <u>The salary</u> of a <u>salaried man</u> is not <u>as higher</u> <u>than that</u> of a lawyer in Korea.
    a)   b)   c)   d)

6. The rock group is performing better <u>as</u> it <u>ever</u> has <u>performed</u> before, everybody
                                    a)   b)   c)

<u>agrees</u>.
   d)

7. <u>When</u> the benefit concert was <u>performed</u>, the crowd <u>was</u> larger <u>when</u>
   a)   b)   c)   d)

anticipated.

8. Because of <u>a higher</u> fuel prices, the <u>preliminary</u> cost estimates <u>need</u> to be
　　　　　 a)　　　　　　　　　　　　　　　 b)　　　　　　　　　　　　 c)

<u>recalculated</u>.
　 d)

1. c) 2. d) 3. b) 4. c) 5. c) 6. a) 7. d) 8. a)　　정답

C. 부사(Adverb)

1. 부사의 기능
　① 동사 수식 : John **gets up early** in the morning.
　② 형용사 수식 : They remained **quite quiet**.
　③ 부사 수식 : It rains **so hard**.
　④ 명사 수식 : **Even Jason** can solve the problem. **Only Jason** told me the
　　　　　　　　 truth.
　⑤ 구 수식 : She told me the truth soon **after her arrival**.(soon이 전치사구
　　　　　　　 를 수식한다.)
　⑥ 문장 수식 : **Frankly, she is not my sister. Happily, they did not die.**
　⑦ 절 수식 : She had arrived **shortly before he left**.

2. 부사의 위치
　1) 수식하는 어구. 절 .문장 앞에 위치
　　They talked **too** much long.(단어수식)/ The came **soon** after dark(구 수식)
　　Foolishly, I talked to him.(문장 수식)
　2) 동사를 수식할 땐 2가지 원칙이 적용됨.
　　(1) 문장의 끝: I talked to him **foolishly**.
　　(2) 의미를 강조할 땐 동사 앞에: I **foolishly** talked to him.

3. 부사의 위치 (Ⅱ)
　1) 빈도·부정 부사: 사건의 횟수나, 행위의 부정을 나타내며 일반 동사 앞,
　　be동사와 조동사 뒤에 온다.

(1) 빈도부사

They often can me. He always does his work well.

부사 예: sometimes, always, usually, often, frequently, ever, generally, regularly.

(2) 부정부사 : He seldom tell me the truth.

부사 예: seldom, barely, hardly, scarcely, never, rarely

(3) enough : enough는 형용사, 부사가 오면 그 뒤에, 명사가 오면 앞에 위치함.

4. 부사의 위치(Ⅲ) (초점부사)

1) 전치 초점 부사 : **Only** Tom said hello to me. **Even** John bought her a new dress.

부사 예 : only, even, also, just, merely, purely, simply, exactly, precisely(정확히), exclusively(오로지~만), solely

2) 후치 초점 부사 : John **alone** visited me today. I had some food, and some wine

부사 예 : alone, too, in particular(특히), either

---

1. The personnel manager sent out the _____ selected resources to the department of advertisements.

a) new   b) newer

c) newly   d) renew

2. In my opinion, each of their products is exceptional well made.
   a)   b)   c)   d)

3. Due to excessive high interest rates, many small businesses are going bankrupt.
   a)   b)   c)   d)

4. The indoor temperature was enough hot to turn on the air conditioner.
     a)   b)   c)   d)

5. A _____ delicate film would best display the scene of importance.

a) corresponding
b) correspondingly
c) correspondent
d) correspondence

6. The chairman of the Board _____ welcomed all of guests.

a) personalize
b) personally
c) personal
d) person

7. The employees who travel abroad frequently are _____ required to get health checkups.

a) routinely
b) obviously
c) quitely
d) overly

8. As a result of _____ wonderful performance of the play the crowd gave the players a standing ovation.

a) exception
b) exceptional
c) exceptionally
d) except

D. 관계부사(Relative Pronoun)

※ 관계부사 = 접속사 + 부사로서 뒤에 완전한 문장이 온다.

This is the house where(=and there) my wife was born.

Summer is a season when(=and then) we can swim.

I don't know the reason why(=and for that) he quit the job.

※ 관계부사 = 전치사 + 관계대명사

This is the place where(=in which) Jason was born.

I know the day when(=on which) the concert was performed.

This is the reason why(= for which) his sweetheart was so upset.

Tell me (the way) how(=in which) you soothed your angry wife.

■ 관계부사의 생략

* Where만 제외하고 관계부사는 생략가능. 또한 선행사도 생략가능.

선행사 the time, the place, the reason, the way 도 생략가능

① Tell him the time when the phone was connected.(○)

  Tell him the time (when) the phone was connected.(○)

  Tell him (the time) when the phone was connected.(○)

② This is the place where we started our business.(○)

  This is the place (where) we started our business.(×)

  This is (the place) where we started our business.(○)

③ This is the reason why I stopped smoking. (○)

  This is the reason (why) I stopped smoking.(○)

  This is (the reason) why I stopped smoking. (○)

④ the way와 how중에서 둘중에 하나는 반드시 생략!

  This is the way how he solves the problem. (×)

  This is (the way) how he solves the problem.(○)

  This is the way (how) he solves the problem.(○)

■ 복합관계부사 : ever와 함께 쓰임."No matter+관계부사"로 바꿀 수 있음.

Come whenever (=at any time when) you want to. = Come no matter when you want to.

Wherever(=at any place where) you go, you will be respected. = No matter where you go, you'll be respected.

However fast you go, you can't arrive in time. = No matter how fast you go, you can't arrive in time.

1. Fire <u>has been</u> used <u>ever</u> <u>since</u> the Stone Age <u>when</u> was found.
   a)   b) c)   d)

2. <u>The number</u> of students <u>whom take</u> to the street is <u>much</u> less than <u>that</u> of
 a)   b)   c)   d)

many years ago.

3. One of the most famous <u>women</u> of the company was the 4th president, her
a)

<u>business policy</u> is <u>very</u> unique & <u>creative</u>.
    b)   c)   d)

4. March is a month _____ people usually expect the weather to change.

  a) for   b) where

  c) during   d) in which

5. <u>Though</u> he deserves <u>recognition for</u> his sales he should <u>know</u> that he is not
  a)   b)   c)

only one <u>whose</u> puts in long hours for sales.
          d)

6. <u>The management</u> of the pizza restaurant announced <u>what</u> they should open <u>at</u>
     a)   b)   c)

11:00 and <u>close</u> at 11:00 p.m.
          d)

7. The president of the company makes her daughter get married to _____

likes his daughter most.

  a) who   b) whomever

  c) whoever   d) whose

8. <u>As</u> managing director he <u>must</u> decide what gets <u>done</u> and by <u>whoever</u>.
  a)   b)   c)   d)

Chapter 8

관사(Article), 전치사(Preposition), 접속사(Conjunction)

A. 관사(Article)

■ 부정 관사의 용법

1. I think him to be a liar. (=one)
2. A bird in the hand is worth two in the bush. (=one)
3. An owl can see in the dark. (=any)
4. A Mr. Brown came to see you yesterday. (=a certain)
5. Birds of a feather flock together. (=the same)
6. He makes it a rule to go there once a week. (=per)
7. They ran out in a hurry.

■ 관용적 표현

all of a sudden, on an average, at a distance, as a rule, once upon a time, come to an end, have a head for ~, have a fancy for ~

■ 정관사의 용법

1. 계량의 단위 표시 : by + the + 단위 표시 명사
   We work by the hour. (우리는 시간제로 일한다.)
2. 신체의 부분을 나타내는 경우
   * catch (or, hold, seize, take) + 사람 + by the 신체 부분 : 「~의 …를 잡다」
   * strike (or, hit, beat, pat) + 사람 + on the 신체 부분 : 「~의 …를 때리다(두드리다)」
   * look (or, stare) + 사람 + in the 신체 부분 : 「~의 …를 보다(응시하다)」
3. 관용적 표현
   Ex. in the shade : 그늘에   in the sun : 양지에

on the increase : 증가하고 있는   to the point : 요령 있는

on the whole : 대체로   in the way : 방해되는

■ 정관사(the)를 붙이는 고유 명사

1. 강, 바다, 운하, 해협 : the Thames, the Pacific (Ocean), the Suez Canal

2. 반도, 산맥, 군도, 복수형의 국명 : the Malay Peninsula, the Alps, the Philippines

3. 신문, 잡지, 서적 : the New York Times, the Reader's Digest, the Bible

4. 공공건물, 관청, 호텔 : the British Museum, the Foreign Office, the Grand Hotel

5. 선박, 철도, 기차, 항공기 : the May Flower, the Gyeongbu(경부선), the KAL(KAL기)

6. 가족 전체, 국민 전체 : the Browns, the Koreans

7. 형용사를 동반한 고유 명사 : the famous Napoleon, the ambitious Caesar

8. 역, 다리, 항구, 호수, 공항, 공원에는 관사가 없다.

■ 관사의 생략

1. Waiter, bring my bill. (호격)

2. Father will come home soon. (가족)

3. (a) Professor Kim is an authority on the subject. (칭호, 관직, 신분)

   (b) Charles Darwin, author of the Origin of Species, died in 1882.

   (c) They elected him mayor of the city.

4. I went to bed early, because I was very tired. (고유목적)

5. Child as he was, he was not afraid. (양보구문)

6. We have breakfast at seven every morning. (식사, 질병, 운동)

   Tobacco will be the cause of cancer.

   We were playing baseball.

7. The bamboo is a kind of grass.

8. Friend and foe lay down side by side. (대조, 반복)

9. I will let you know the result by telephone.

   He never gave way to temptation.

■ 관용적 표현

• 교통, 통신 수단 : by train, on foot, by letter

• 기타 : take place, have fun, without fail

B. 전치사(Preposition) I

▪ 전치사

전치사는 글자그대로 "앞에 둔다"는 뜻이다. 전치사는 명사상당어귀 앞에 둔다.

1. **at**

① 짧은 시각 시점 등에서 at 9 o'clock, at dawn, at noon, at night, at the end(beginning) of May

② 한 지점에(좁은공간)

I met her at the corner.(코너에서)

He lives at 2233 highland Road.(2233번지에)

Our train is going at 70miles an hour.(시속 70마일로)

He is at breakfast now. (at breakfast: 종사의 at)

2. **in**

세기, 년, 월, 계절, 오전, 오후 등 비교적 긴 시간에/ 넓은 공간이나 장소/ …만에, …후에

in March, in summer, in the 21st century, in the afternoon, in the evening, in the middle of night, in this city, in Korea

He cleaned his room in one hour.

I'll start for L.A. in three days.

3. **on**

① 날짜, 요일, 특정한 날(아침, 오후, 밤)등에 쓰임.

My birthday is on June 15(th).

He came here on Monday, but he left for L.A. on the next day.

He experienced a car accident on a foggy night.

② (선·면에 접속해), ~위에 (반대표현, off)

She is sitting on a chair. Many apples are hanging on the tree.

The house is on fire. (on fire : 불이 붙다)

He is on another line. (전화의 접속)

He is on duty. (책임의, 근무하는)

All the drinks are on me. (책임지는, 지불하는)

All the drinks are on the house. (주최측이 내는)

4. **until** 및 **by** : until은 어떤 시점까지의 동작 및 상태의 계속 by는 어느 시점까지의 동작 및 상태의 완료

   Study hard until 10 O'clock for your final exam. Let's meet there by 10 O'clock.

5. **after ~후에** (*in은 미래시제를 중심으로 함.)

   He left here after two days.

   He thought that he would leave here in two days.

6. **within ~이내에**

   He'll come back home within two weeks.

7. **for ~동안에/ during ~동안에**

   for다음에는 구체적 기간 즉, 숫자가 옴. during은 구체적이지 않는 기간이며 while의 뜻임.

   For five days I didn't have anything. During a few days I didn't have anything.

   Her husband gave her good care while she was pregnant/ during her pregnancy.

8. **원인·이유**

   because of·on account of·owing[due] to·thanks to : 직접적인 원인
   Because of the rain, the ground was wet.
   He closed the factory on account of his poor health.
   We had a bad accident owing[due] [thanks] to careless driving.
   Out of·From: 동기 She did it out of pity. (그녀는 동정심에 그렇게 했다.)
   His failure resulted from laziness. (result from: ~에서 기인하다)

9. **양보**

   in spite of, for all, with all, despite, notwithstanding ~에도 불구하고
   He went to school in spite of his sickness.
   For all [With all] his efforts, he couldn't succeed.
   Despite his illness, he went to work.
   Notwithstanding her remarks, she is very clever.

10. **관계·참조**

   with regard to, regarding, as regards, in respect to, with respect to, concerning ~에 관하여

I have nothing to say with regard to [regarding·as regards·in respect to, with respect to, concerning] marriage.

As for[As to] the journey, we'll decide that later.

She carried out her plan regardless of expense. (그녀는 비용에 관계없이 계획을 수행했다.)

1. It was said that the Director's meeting began _____ Sept. 3rd.
   a) at
   b) with
   c) on
   d) over

2. We made a decision to have a meeting on 10 o'clock for receiving orders.
           a)   b)   c)   d)

3. The task must be carried out _____ next Tuesday.
   a) to
   b) until
   c) by
   d) when

4. When I tried to talk to him on the phone he was _____ study.
   a) in
   b) for
   c) at
   d) with

5. _____ the new management, the fringe benefit will go through any cutdown.
   a) Over
   b) Under
   c) Between
   d) Towards

6. Except the weather is bad, every thing is prepared for us to go on a picnic.
     a)   b)   c)   d)

7. It is known that the Main Road will be _____ construction until next Friday.
   a) by
   b) under
   c) in
   d) on

8. It is said that the city museum will open _____ 8. p.m.

    a) until   b) by

    c) through   d) on

9. Despite he exerts much efforts to get the driver's license, it was useless in the

    a)   b)   c)   d)

end.

10. _____ labor negotiations, all vacations had to be put off.

    a) Because   b) Due to

    c) As   d) During for

11. He is second to none _____ English among his colleagues.

    a) at   b) as of

    c) concerning   d) with regarding

12. In spite he hurried to apply for the position, he couldn't meet the deadline.

    a)   b)   c)   d)

13. He insisted on coming with them despite of deteriorating weather condition in

             a)   b)   c)   d)

the downtown.

14. Because the extensive efforts of gaining recognition from Johnson Inc, we

    a)   b)   c)

could take the order from the company.

               d)

15. When he has to shop for groceries he always stops by the store nearing his

         a)   b)   c)   d)

house.

1. c)　2. b)　3. c)　4. c)　5. b)　6. a)　7. b)　8. a)　9. a) 10. b)
11. c) 12. a) 13. b) 14. a) 15. d)

정답

C. 접속사(Conjunction)

■ 등위접속사

대등한 관계에 있는 단어, 구, 절을 연결하는 말, and, but, or 등이 있음.

- and : 동시성/연속성/결과/대조

  He drove his car and drank mineral water.

  He phoned Mary and talked to her.

  He was sick and saw a doctor.

- but : 대조/(앞문장의 부정어와 함께)대구

  He is poor but cheerful.

  It is not red, but yellow.

  He didn't go to school, but stayed at home.

- or : 선택(어구나 절을 연결)

  John or I have to stay there.

  Which do you like better, A course or B?

  * Go at once or you will miss the train.(명령문 + or 「~해라 그러면 …」)

■ 종속접속사

종속절을 이끄는 접속사로, 주절+명사절, 형용사절, 부사절로 나눔.
다시 부사절은 의미상으로 시간, 이유, 조건, 양보, 목적, 양태로 나눔.

- 명사절

  That he will succeed is certain.(=It is certain that he will succeed.)

  Do you know when that happened?

- 형용사절

  She is the fund manager whom you can trust.

  Tell me the truth which you cherish in your heart.

- 부사절

  He waved when he saw her.

  He was absent because he was sick. If he fails, he will do it again.

  Though he is young, he is wise.

  He came to the library in order that he could lend out some books.

  Take things as they are. (사물을 있는 그대로 받아들여라.)

1. He neither drinks, smokes, _____ eats large meals to go on a diet.

   a) or   b) nor

   c) and   d) but

2. He will <u>continue</u> to <u>participate in</u> professional sports <u>although</u> his <u>injuries</u>.
                a)   b)   c)   d)

3. They went home as _____ as they finished their task.

   a) much   b) soon

   c) good   d) many

4. Their products are known not only for their price, _____ for their quality.

    a) never

    b) but also

    c) and also

    d) as well as

5. _____ he is known to only a few as a novelist, his reputation among them is very great.

    a) Because

    b) Although

    c) Even

    d) For

6. Your answers to the questions are essential for our service files _____ will give hands to us in serving you more efficiently.

    a) because

    b) so

    c) however

    d) and

7. <u>Except</u> the weather is bad, <u>every</u> thing <u>is</u> prepared for us to go <u>on</u> a picnic.
    a)   b)   c)   d)

8. Turn in the report by tomorrow without fail, _____, the professor will not give you your grade.

    a) otherwise

    b) by

    c) for

    d) unless

1. b)　2. c)　3. b)　4. b)　5. b)　6. d)　7. b)　8. a)　정답

PART 3

· · ·

번역 자료

① The Gift of Understanding

Paul Villiard

I must have been[1] around four years old when I first entered Mr. Wigden's candy shop, but the smell of that wonderful world of penny treasures[2] still comes back to me clearly more than half-century later. Whenever he heard the tiny tinkle of the bell attached to[3] the front door, Mr. Wigden quietly appeared, to take his stand[4] behind the candy case. He was very old, and his head was topped with a cloud of fine, snow-white hair.[5]

Never was such an array of delicious temptations spread before a child.[6] It was almost painful to make a choice. Each kind had first to be savored in the imagination before passing on to the next. There was always a short pang of regret as the selection was dropped into a little white paper sack. Perhaps another kind would taste better? Or last longer? Mr. Wigden had a trick of scooping your selection into the sack, then pausing. `Not a word was spoken, but every child understood that Mr. Wigden's raised eyebrows constituted a last minute opportunity[7] to make an exchange. Only after payment was laid upon the counter was the sack irrevocably[8] twisted shut and the moment of indecision[9] ended.

Our house was two blocks from the streetcar line, and you had to pass the shop going to and from the cars. Mother had taken me into town on some forgotten errand, and as we walked home from the trolley Mother turned into[10] Mr. Wigden's

"Let's see if we can find something good." she said, leading me up to the long glass case as the old man approached from behind a curtained aperture.[11] My mother stood talking with him for a few minutes as I gazed rapturously at the display[12] before my eyes. Finally Mother picked out something for me and paid Mr. Wigden.

Mother went into town once or twice a week, and since in those days baby-sitters were almost unheard-of, I usually accompanied her. It became a regular routine for her to take me into the candy shop for some special treat,[13] and after that first visit I was always allowed to make my own choice.

I knew nothing of money at that time. I would watch my mother hand something to people, who would then hand her a package or a bag, and slowly the idea of exchange percolated into my mind.[14] Sometime about then I reached a decision. I would journey the interminable[15] two blocks to Mr. Wigden's all alone. I remember the tinkle of the bell as I managed, after some considerable effort,[16] to push open the big door, Enthralled, I worked my way slowly down the display counter.[17]

Here were spearmint leaves with a fresh minty fragrance.[18] There, gumdrops[19]— the great big ones, so tender to bite into, all crusty with crystals of sugar. In the next tray were fudgy[20] chocolate babies.[21] The next behind them held enormous jawbreakers[22] which made a satisfying bulge in your cheek. The hard, shiny, dark-brown-covered peanuts Mr. Wigden dished out[23] with a little scoop—tow scoops for a cent. And, of course, there were the licorice whips.[24] These lasted a long time if you let the bites dissolve instead of chewing them.

When I had picked our a promising assortment,[25] Mr. Wigden leaned over and asked, "You have the money to pay for all these?"

"Oh, yes," I replied, "I have lots of money." I reached outr my fist, and into Mr. Wigden's open hand I dumped a half-odozen cherry seeds carefully wrapped in shiny tinfoil

Mr. Wigden stood gazing at the palm of his hand ; then he looked searchingly at[26] me for a long moment.

"Isn't it enough?" I asked him anxiously.

He sighed gently. "I think it is a bit too much," he answered. "You have some change coming." He walked overto his oldfashioned cash register and cranked open the drawer. Returning to the counter, he leaned over and dropped two pennies into my oustretched hand.

My mother scolded me about taking the trip[27] alone when she found me out. I don't think it ever occurred to[28] her to ask about the financial arrangement.[29] I must have obeyed and, evidently, when permission was granted for me to make the trip, a cent or two was given me for my purchases, since I don't remember using cherry seeds a second time.[30] In fact, the whole affair, insignificant to me then, was soon forgotten in the busy occupation of growing up.[31]

When I was six or seven years old my family moved east, where I grew up, eventually married and established my own family. My wife and I opened a shop where we bred and sold exotic fish. The aquarium trade[32] was then still in its infancy,[33] and most of the fish were imported directly from Asia, Africa and South America. Few species sold for less than five dollars a pair.[34]

One sunny afternoon a little girl came in accompanied by her brother. They were perhaps five and six years old. I was busy cleaning the tanks. The two children stood with wide, round eyes, staring at the jeweled beauties[35] swimming in the crystal-clear water. "Gosh," exclaimed the boy, "can we buy some?"

"Yes," I replied. "If you can pay for them."

"Oh, we have lots of money," the little girl said confidently.

Something in the way she spoke gave me an odd feeling of familiarity.[36] After watching the fish for some time, they asked me for pairs of several different kinds, pointing them out as they walked down the row of tanks. I netted their choices into a traveling container[37] and slipped in into an insulated bag for transport, handing it to the boy. "Carry it carefully," I cautioned.

He nodded and turned to his sister. "You pay him," he said. I held out my hand, and as her clenched fist approached me. I suddenly knew exactly what was going to happen, even what the little girl was going to say. Her fist opened, and into my outstretched palm she dumped two nickels and a dime.

At that instant I sensed the full impact of the legacy[38] Mr. Wigden had given me so many years before Only now did I recognize the challenge I had presented the old man, and realize how wonderfully he had met[39] it.

I seemed to be standing again in the little candy shop as I looked at the coins in my own hand. I understood the innocence of the two children and the power to preserve or destroy that innocence, as Mr. Wigden had understood those long years ago. I was so filled up with the remembering that my throat ached. The little girl was standing expectantly before me. "Isn't it enough?" she asked in a small voice.

"It's a little too much," I managed to say, somehow, over the lump in my throat.[40] "You have some change coming." I rummaged around[41] in the cash drawer, dropped two pennies into her open hand, then stood in the doorway watching the children go down the walk carefully carrying their treasure.

When I turned back into shop, my wife was standing on a stool with her arms submerged to the elbows in a tank where she was rearranging the plants. "Mind telling me what that was all about?" she asked. "Do you know how many fish you gave them?"

"About 30 dollars' worth," I answered, the lump still in my throat. "But I couldn't have done anything else."

When I'd finished telling her about old Mr. Wigden, her eyes were wet, and she stepped off the stool and gave me a gentle kiss on the cheek.

"I still smell the gumdrops," I sighed, and I'm certain I heard old Mr. Wigden chuckle over my shoulder as I swabbed[42] down the last tank.

1) must have been: ~이었음에 틀림이 없다(과거사실에 대한 추측 판단)

2) penny treasures: 푼돈으로 살 수 있는 보석같은 사탕들

3) attached to: ~에 부착된 , attached 앞에 which was를 보충해 볼 것

4) take one's stand: 자리잡다

5) a cloud of fine, snow-white hair: 눈처럼 희고 숱이 많은 멋진 머리카락

6) Never… a child: Such an array of delicious temptations was never spread before a child의 문장이 정치구문임

7) constitute a last-minute opportunity: 마지막 기회가 되다

8) irrevocably: 되물릴 수 없도록, 취소할 수 없게

9) the moment of indecision: 망설임의 순간

10) turn into: stop at, drop into, 들르다

11) from behind a curtained aperture: 커튼친 틈 뒤에서

12) gaze rapturously at: 넋을 놓고 바라보다
     display: 진열된 상품

13) for some special treat: 특별히 한턱 내려고, 구슬리기 위한 특별한 대접을 위하여

14) percolate into my mind: 생각속에 자리잡다, 개념이 잡히다

15) interminable: endless 끝없는, 아주 먼

16) after some special effort: 상당히 애쓴 후

17) work one's way: 애써 나아가다 / display counter: 진열대

18) spearmint leaves with a fresh minty fragrance: 신선한 박하향이 나는 얇은 잎파리 모양의 박하 과자들.

19) gumdrop: jellylike candy

20) fudgy: (우유 설탕, 초콜렛으로 만든 부드러운) 캔디같은
     cf. fudge: 허튼소리, 꾸며낸 이야기. 신문의 따로 인쇄한 추가 기사.

21) chocolate baby: 조그마한 초콜렛

22) jawbreaker: 딱딱한 사탕, 큰 사탕

23) dish out: 퍼담다, 목적어는 The hard, shiny, dark-drown-covered peanuts

24) licorice whip: 감초를 섞어 거품을 내서 만든 과자

25) pick out a promising assortment: 맛있으리라고 기대되는 여러 가지 것을 구색을 맞추어 고르다

26) look searchingly at: 뚫어지게 쳐다보다

27) taking the trip: 여행한 일, 여기서는 혼자 사탕가게에 간 일

28) occur to: (머리에)떠오르다, 생각이 나다

29) financial arrngement: 재정적 처리, 돈 문제

30) a second time: again

31) in the busy occupation of growing up: 성장의 와중에

32) aquarium trade: 수족관 사업

33) in one's infancy: 초창기

34) Few species ~a pair: 어떠한 종류의 것들이나 한 쌍에 5달러 아래로 팔리는 것은 거의 없다.

35) jeweled beauties: jewel fish: 보석같이 아름다운 열대어들

36) odd feeling of familiarity: 이상한 친근감

37) traveling container: 휴대용기

38) the full impact of the legacy: 유산의 완전한 효과, 영향

39) meet: cope with 대처하다

40) over the lump in my throat: 목 메인 것을 참고

41) rummage around: (샅샅이)뒤지다, 수색하다

42) swab: 걸레질하다

Dear Dad,
Gue$$ what I need mo$t of all. That' $ right.
Plea$e $end me $ome $oon. Be$t wihe.
Your $on $am

Dear Sam
NOthing much has happened lately. Glad to kNOw you like your school,
Write us aNOther letter. NOw I must say goodbye; just wanted to send a
NOte.
Your Dad.

2 Désirée's Baby

Kate Chopin[*]

As the day was pleasant, Madame Valmondé drove over to L'Abri[1)] to see Désirée and the baby.

It made her laugh to think of Désirée with a baby. Why, it seemed but yesterday that Désirée was little more than[2)] a baby herself ; when Monsieur in riding through the gateway of Valmondé had found her lying asleep in the shadow of the big stone pillar.

The little one awoke in his arms and began to cry for "Dada." That was as much as she could do or say, Some people thought she might have strayed there of her own accord,[3)] for she was of the toddling age.[4)] The prevailing belief was that she had been purposely left by a party of Texans, whose canvas-covered wagon, late in the day, had crossed the ferry that Coton Ma☐ s kept, just below the plantation. In time Madame Valmondé abandoned every speculation but the one that Désirée had been sent to her by a beneficent Providence to be the child of her affection, seeing that she was without child of the flesh. For the girl grew to be beautiful and gentle, affectionate and sincere— the idol of Valmondé.

It was no wonder, when she stood one day against the stone pillar in whose shadow she had lain asleep, eighteen years before, that Armand Aubigny, riding by and seeing her there, had fallen in love with her. That was the way all the Aubignys fell in love, as if struck by a pistol shot.[5)] The wonder was that he had not loved her before ; for he had known her since his father brought him home from Paris, a boy of eight, after his mother died there. The passion that awoke in him that day, when he saw her at the gate, swept along like an avalanche, or like a prairie fire, or like anything that drives headlong over all obstacles.

Monsieur Valmondé grew practical and wanted things well considered : that is, the girl's obscure origin. Armand looked into her eyes and did not care. He was reminded that she was nameless. What did it matter about a name when he could give her one of the oldest and proudest in Louisiana? He ordered the corbeille[6] from Paris, and contained himself with what patience he could until it arrived ; then they were married.

Madame Valmondé had not seen Désirée and the baby for four weeks. When she reached L'Abri she shuddered at the first sight of it, as she always did. It was a sad looking place, which for many years had not known the gentle presence of a mistress ; old Monsieur Aubigny having married and buried his wife in France, as she having loved her own land too well ever to leave it. The roof came down steep and black like a cowl, reaching our beyond the wide galleries that encircled the yellow stuccoed house, Big, solemn oaks grew close to it, and their thick-leaved, far-reaching branches shadowed it like a pall. Young Aubigny's rule was a strict one, too, and under it his Negroes had forgotten how to be gay, as they had been during the old master's easy-going and indulgent[7] lifetime.

The young mother was recovering slowly, and lay full length, in her soft white muslins and laces, upon a couch. The baby was beside her, upon her arm, where he had fallen asleep, at her breast. The yellow nurse woman sat beside a window fanning herself.

Madame Valmondé bent her portly figure over Désirée and kissed her, holding her an instant tenderly in her arms, Then she turned to the child.

"This is not the baby!" she exclaimed in startled tones. French was the language spoken at Valmondé in those days.

"I knew you would be astonished," laughed Desirée, "at the way has grown. The little cochen de lait![8] Look at his legs, Mama, and his hands and fingernails—real fingernails. Zandrine had to cut them this morning. Isn't it true, Zandrine?"

The woman bowed her turbaned head majestically, "Mais si, Mdame."

"And the way he cries," went on Desirée, "is deafening. Armand heard him the other day as far away as La Blanche's cabin."

Madame Valmondé had never removed her eyes from the child. She lifted it and walked with it to the window that was lightest. She scanned the baby narrowly,[9] then looked searchingly at Zandrine, whose face was turned to gaze across the fields.

"Yes, the child has grown, has changed," said Madame Valmondé, slowly, as she replaced it beside its mother. "What does Armand say?"

Desirée's face became suffused with a glow that was happiness itself.

"Oh, Armand is the proudest father in the parish, I believe, chiefly because it is a boy, to bear his name ; though he says not—that he would have loved a girl as well. But I know it isn't true. I know he says that to please me. And Mama," she added, drawing Madame Valmondé's head down to her, and speaking in a whisper, "he hasn't punished one of them—not one of them—since baby is born. Even Negrillon, who pretended to have burnt his leg that he might rest from work—he only laughed, and said Negrillon was a great scamp. Oh, Mama, I'm so happy ; it frightens me."

What Desirée said was true. Marriage, and later the birth of his son, had softened Armand Aubigny's imperious and exacting nature greatly. This was what made the gentle Desirée so happy for she loved him desperately. When he forwned she trembled, but loved him. When he frowned she trembled, but loved him. When he smiled, she asked no greater blessing of God. But Armand's dark, handsome face had not been disfigured by frowns since the day he fell in love with her.

When the baby was about three months old, Dèsirèe awoke one day to the conviction that there was something in the air[10] menacing her peace. It was at first too subtle to grasp. It had only been a disquieting[11] suggestion ; an air of mystery among the blacks ; unexpected visits from far-off neighbors who could hardly account for their coming. Then a strange, an awful change in her husband's manner, which she dared not ask him to explain. When he spoke to her, it was with averted eyes, from which the old love-light seemed to have gone our. He absented himself from home ; and when there, avoided her presence and that of her child, without excuse. And the very spirit of Satan[12] seemed suddenly to take hold of him in his dealings with the slaves. Dèsirèe was miserable enough to die.

She sat in her room, one hot afternoon, in her peignoir,[13] listlessly drawing through her fingers the strands of her long, silky brown hair that hung about her shoulders. The baby, half naked, lay asleep upon her own great mahogany bed, that was like a sumptuous[14] throne, with its satin-lined half-canopy. One of La Blanche's little quadroon[15] boys—half naked too—stood fanning the child slowly with a fan of peacock feathers. Dèsirèe's eyes had been fixed absently and sadly upon the baby, while she was striving to penetrate the threatening mist that she felt was closing about her. She looked from her child to the boy who stood beside him, and back again ; over and over. "Ah!" It was a cry that she could not help : which she was not conscious of having uttered. The blood turned like ice in her veins, and a clammy[16] moisture gathered upon her face.

She tried to speak to the little quadroon boy ; but no sound would come at first. When he heard his name uttered, he looked up, and his mistress was pointing to the door. He laid aside the great, soft fan, and obediently stole away over the polished floor, on his bare tiptoes.

She stayed motionless, with gaze riveted upon her child, and her face the picture of fright.

Presently her husband entered the room, and without noticing her, went to a table and began to search among some papers which covered it.

"Armand," she panted once more, "look at our child. What does it mean? Tell me."

He coldly but gently loosened her fingers from about his arm and thrust her hand away from him. "Tell me what it means!" she cried despairingly.

"It means," he answered lightly, "that the child is not white; it means that you are not white."

A quick conception of all that this accusation meant for her nerved[17] her with unwonted[18] courage to deny it. "It is a lie ; it is not true. I am white! Look at my hair, it is brown ; and my eyes are grey, Armand, you know they are grey. And my skin is fair," seizing his wrist, Look at my hand ; whiter than yours, Armand, she laughed hysterically.

"As white as La Blanche's" he returned cruelly ; and went away leaving her alone with their child.

When she could hold a pen in her hand, she sent a despairing letter to Madame Valmondé.

"My mother, they tell me I am not white. Armand has told me that I am not white. For God's sake tell them it is not true. You must know it is not true. I shall die. I must die. I cannot be so unhappy, and live."

The answer that came was brief :

"My own Désirée : Come home to Valmondé ; back to your mother who loves you. Come with your child."

When the letter reached Désirée, she went with it to her husband's study, and laid it upon the desk before which he sat. She was like a stone image : silent, white, motionless after she placed it there.

In silence he ran his cold eyes over the written words. He said nothing.

"Shall I go, Armand?" she asked in tones sharp with agonized suspense.

"Yes, go."

"Do you want me to go?"

"Yes, I want you to go."

He thought Almighty God had dealt cruelly and unjustly with him ; and felt, somehow, that he was paying Him back in kind[19] when he stabbed thus into his wife's soul. Moreover he no longer loved her, because of the unconscious injury she had brought upon his home and his name.

She turned away like one stunned by a blow, and walked slowly towards the door, hoping he would call her back.

"Good-by, Armand," she moaned.

He did not answer her. That was his last blow at fate.[20]

Desirée went in search of her child. Zandrine was pacing the somber gallery with it. She took the little one from the nurse's arms with no word of explanation, and descending the steps, walked away, under the live-oak branches.

It was an October afternoon ; the sun was just sinking. Out in the still fields the Negroes were picking cotten.

Desirée had not changed the thin white garment nor the slippers which she wore. Her hair was uncovered and the sun's rays brought a golden gleam from its brown meshes. She did not take the broad, beaten road which led to the far-off plantation of Valmondé. She walked across a deserted field, where the stubble bruised her tender feet, so delicately shod, and tore her thin gown to shreds.

She disappeared among the reeds and willows that grew thick along the banks of the deep, sluggish[21] bayou :and she did not come back again.

Some weeks later there was a curious scene enacted at L'abri. In the center of the smoothly swept back yard was a great bonfire. Armand Aubigny sat in the wide hallway that commanded a view of the spectacle ; and it was he who dealt out to half a dozen Negroes the material which kept this fire ablaze.

A graceful cradle of willow, with all its dainty furbishings[22], was laid upon the pyre,[23] which had already been fed with the richness of a priceless layette.[24] Then there were silk gowns, and velvet and satin ones added to these ; laces, too, and embroideries ; bonnets and gloves ; for the corbeille had been of rare quality.

The last thing to go was a tiny bundle of letters ; innocent little scribblings that Désirée had sent to him during the days of their espousal. There was the remnant of one back in the drawer from which he took them. But it was not Désirée's ; it was part of an old letter from his mother to his father. He read it. she was thanking God for the blessing of her husband's love :

"But, above all," she worte, "night and day, I thank the good God for having so arranged our lives that our dear Armand will never know that his mother, who adores him, belongs to the race that is cursed with the brand of slavery."

Footnotes

* Kate Chopin (Katherine O'Faherty Chopin) ; 1851 - 1904 ; Kate O'Flaherty was born in St Louis, of an Irish father and a French mother, and went to live in New Orleans when she married Oscar Chopin took over a Louisiana cotton plantation but he died of swamp fever when Kate was 31. She found the management of the plantation too demanding and after two years returned to St Louis with her son, Jean, and turned to writing. She wrote occasional pieces, stories for children, and a play ; she published a novel, At Fault (1890), which was not a success but which demonstrated her skill at evoking the Creole and Cajun backgrounds of her life in Louisiana.

1) L' Abri: 라브리 농장.

2) little more than: as good as

3) of her own accord: 자발적으로

4) of toddling age: 걸음마 하는 나이

5) as if struck by a pistol shot: 전격적으로.

6) corbeille(불): 결혼 선물.

7) indulgent: 관대한(lenient)

8) cochin de lait(불): 젖꿀꿀이 (젖 많이 먹는 애기를 비유)

9) scanned the baby narrowly: 아기를 세밀히 관찰하다.

10) something in the air: 뭔가 분위기가.

11) disquieting: 불안한

12) the very spirit of Satan: 악령 그 자체, 즉 심한 cruelty를 뜻함.

13) peignoir(불): 부인용 실내복.

14) sumptuous: looking expensive

15) quadroon: 백인과 mulatto (반백인)과의 혼혈인, 즉 흑인의 피를 1/4 받은 사람.

16) clammy: 끈적끈적한

17) nerved: encouraged.

18) unwonted: unusual

19) in kind: 같은 방법으로

20) That was his last blow at fate: 그가 운명에 가한 최후의 강타였다. 즉 끝까지 cruel 했음을 의미.

21) sluggish: slow moving

22) furbishings: 장식

23) pyre: large pile of wood

24) layette(불): 갓난아이의 용품(옷, 따위)

A young boy and his doting grandmother were walking along the shore in Miami Beach when a huge wave appeared out of nowhere, sweeping the child lout to sea. The horrified woman fell to her knees, raised her eyes to the heavens and begged the Lord to return her beloved grandson. And, lo, another wave reared up and deposited the stunned child on the sand before her. The grandmother looked the boy over carefully. He was fine. But still she stared up angrily toward the heavens. "When we came," she snapped indignantly, "he had a hat!"

3 Appointment with Love

S. I. Kishor[*]

Six minutes to six, said the great round clock over the information booth in Grand Central Station.[1] The tall young Army lieutenant[2] who had just come from the direction of the tracks lifted his sunburned face, and his eyes narrowed to note the exact time. His heart was pounding with a beat that shocked him because he could not control it. In six minutes, he would see the woman who had fille such a special place in his life for the past thirteen months, the woman he had never seen, yet whose written words had been with him and sustained him unfailingly.[3]

He placed himself as close as he could to the information booth, just beyond the ring of people besieging the clerks.

Lieutenant Blandford remembered one night in particular, the worst of the fighting, w hen his plane had been caught in the midst of a pack of Zeros.[4] He had seen the grinning face of one of the Jap[5] pilots.

In one of his letters, he had confessed to her that he often felt fear, and only a few days before this battle, he had received her answer : "Of course, you fear ⋯ all brave men do. Didn't King David[6] know fear? That's why he wrote the Twenty-third Psalm.[7] Next time you doubt yourself I want you to hear my voice reciting to you : "Yea, though I walk in the valley of the shadow of death, I shall fear no evil, for Thou art with me[8]⋯" And he had remembered : he had heard her imagined voice, and it had renewed his strength and skill.

Now he was going to hear her real voice. Four minutes to six. His face grew sharp.

Under the immense, starred roof,[9] people were walking fast, like threads of color being woven into a gray web. A girl passed close to him, and Lieutenant Blandford started. She was wearing a red flower in her suit lapel, but it was a crimson sweetpea, not the little red rose they had agreed upon. Besides, this girl was too young, about eighteen, whereas Hollis Meynell had frankly told him she was thirty. "Well, what of it ?" he had answered. "I'm thirty-two," He was twenty-nine.

His mind went back to that book—the book the Lord Himself must have put into his hands out of the hundreds of Army library books sent to the Florida[10] training camp. Of Human Bondage,[11] it was ; and throughout the book were notes in a woman's writing. He had always hated that writing-in habit, but these remarks were different. He had never believed that a woman could see into a man's heart so tenderly, so understandingly. Her name was on the bookplate : Hollis Meynell. He had got hold of a New York City telephone book and found her address. He had written, she had answered. Next day he had been shipped out, but they had gone on writing.

For thirteen months, she had faithfully replied, and more than replied. When his letters did not arrive, she wrote anyway, and now he believed he loved her, and she loved him.

But she had refused all his pleas to send him her photograph. That seemed rather bad, of course. But she had explained : "If your feeling for me has any reality, any honest basis, what I look like won't matter. Suppose I'm beautiful. I'd always be haunted by the feeling that you had been taking a chance on just that,[12] and that kind of love would disgust me. Suppose I'm plain[13] (and you must admit that this is more likely) then I'd always fear that you were only going on writing to me because you were lonely and had no one else. No, don't ask for my picture. When you come to New York, you shall see me and then you shall make your decision. Remember, both of us are free to stop or to go on after that—whichever we choose …"

One minute to six … he pulled hard on a cigarette.

Then Lieutenant Blanford's heart leaped higher than his plane had ever done.

A young woman was coming toward him. Her figure was long and slim ; her blonde hair lay back in curls from her delicate ears. Her eyes were blue as flowers, her lips and chin had a gentle firmness. In her pale green suit, she was like springtime come alive.[14]

He started toward her, entirely forgetting to notice that she was wearing no rose, and as he moved, a small, provocative smile curved he lips.

"Going my way,[15] soldier?" she murmured.

Uncontrollably, he made one step closer to her. Then he saw Hollis Meynell.

She was standing almost directly behind the girl, a woman well past forty, her graying hair tucked under a worn hat. She was more than plump ; her thick-ankled feet were thrust into low-heeled shoes. But she wore a red rose in the rumpled brown lapel of her coat.

The girl in the green suit was walking quickly away.

Blandford felt as though he were being split in two, so keen was his desire to follow the girl, yet so deep was his longing for the woman whose spirit had truly companioned and upheld his own ; and there she stood. Her pale, plump face was gentle and sensible ; he could see that now. Her gray eyes had a warm, kindly twinkle.

Lieutenant Blandford did not hesitate. His fingers gripped the small, worn, blue leather copy of Of Human Bondage which was to identify him to her. This would not be love, but it would be something precious, something perhaps even rarer than love — a friendship for which he had been and must ever be grateful …

He squared his broad shoulders, saluted and held the book out toward the woman, although even while he spoke he felt choked by the bitterness of his diappointment.

"I'm Lieutenant John Blandford, and you—you are Miss Meynell. I'm so glad you could meet me. May—may I take you to dinner?"

The woman's face broadened in a tolerant smile. "I don't know what this is all about, son," she answered. "That young lady in the green suit, who just went by, she begged me to wear this rose on my coat. And she said that if you asked me to go out with you, I should tell you that she's waiting for you in that big restaurant across the street. She said it was some kind of a test. I've got[16] two boys with Uncle Sam[17] myself, so I didn't mind to oblige you."[18]

Footnotes

....

* S. I. Kishor: An American short-story writer.

1) Grand Central Station: a terminal station in Upper Manhattan, New York
2) lieutenant: [lefténənt] ; Am. [lu: ténənt;lju: ténənt]
3) unfailingly: at all times
4) zeros: 2차 대전때 일본군이 사용한 전투기의 제작년대 2600(=1940)년의 0자를 딴 것.
5) Jap: Japanse
6) King David: in the Bible, the second king of Israel and Judah ; succeding Saul and followed by his son Solomon ; the reputed writer of the Psalms
7) Psalm: [sa: m]
8) 'Yea, though I walk … with me': Psalm 23.4 ; Yea, though I walk in the valley of the shadow of death, I will fear no evil, for Thou art with me ; Thy rod and Thy staff they comfort me
9) the immense, starred roof: the big roof of the Central Station illuminated with many lights

10) **Florida:** a state on a peninsula in the southeastern United States

11) **Of Human Bondage:** an autobiographical novel by William S. Maugham

12) **just that:** the fact that I am beautiful

13) **plain:** not good-looking ; homely : not beautiful

14) **like springtime come alive:** like springtime which had just come alive

15) **go one's way:** depart, Do you mind going~? 나와 동행하겠어요.

16) **I've got:** I have

17) **Uncle Sam:** an imaginary character supposed to represent the American government :
미국 정부의 속칭

18) **to lblige you:** doing a favor for you

The ardent honeymooning of her 75-year-old groom was exhausting the young bride. During a momentary lull while he was shaving, she staggered down to the coffee shop.

"What's the matter with you, dearie?" asked the waitress.

"Here you are a young bride with an older husband, and you're the one who looks beat."

Said the bride, "That man double-crossed me. He told me he saved up for sixty years, and I thought he was talking about money."

4 Mr. Know-All

*William S. Maugham**

I was prepared to dislike[1] Max Kelada even before I knew him. The war had just finished and the passenger traffic in ocean-going liners[2] was heavy. Accommodation[3] was very hard to get and you had to put up with whatever the agents chose to offer you. You could not hope for a cabin to yourself[4] and I was thankful to be given one in which there were only two berths. but when I was told the name of my companion my heart sank. It suggested closed port-holes[5] and the night air rigidly excluded. It was bad enough to share a cabin for fourteen days with anyone(I was going from San Francisco to Yokohama[6], but I should have looked upon it with less dismay if my fellow- passenger's name had been Smith or Brown.[7]

When I went on board I found Mr. Kelada's luggage already below.[8] I did not like the look of it ; there were too many labels on the suitcases, and the wardrobe trunk was too big. He had unpacked his toilet things, and I observed that he was a partron of the excellent Monsieur Coty;[9] for I saw on the washing-stand his scent, his hair-wash and his brilliantine.[10] Mr. Kelada's brushes, ebony with his monogram in gold, would have been all the better for a scrub. I did not at all like Mr. Kelada. I made my way into the smoking-room. I called for a pack of cards and began to play patience.[11] I had scarecly started before a man came up to me and asked me if he was right in thinking my name was so-and-so.

"I am Mr. Kelada," he added, with a smile that showed a row of flashing teeth, and sat down.

"Oh, yes, we're sharing a cabin, I think."

"Bit of luck, I call it. You never know who you're going to be put in with. I was jolly glad when I heard you were English. I'm all for us English sticking together[12] when we're abroad, if you understand what I mean."

I blinked.

"Are you English?" I asked. perhaps tactlessly.

"Rather. You don't think I look like an American, do you? British to the backbone, that's what I am."

To prove it, Mr. Kelada took out of his pocket a passport and airily[13] waved it under my nose.

King George has many strange subjects.[14] Mr. Kelada was short and of a sturdy build, clean-shaven and dark-skinned, with a fleshy, hooked nose and very large, lustrous and liquid eyes. His long black hair was sleek and curly. He spoke with a fluency in which there was nothing English[15] and his gestures were exuberant.[16] I felt pretty sure that a closer inspection of that British passport would have betrayed the fact that Mr. Kelada was born under a bluer sky[17] than is generally seen in England.

"What will you have?" he asked me.

I looked at him doubtfully. Prohibition[18] was in force[19] and to all appearances the ship was bone-dry.[20] When I am not thirsty I do not know which I dislike more, ginger-ale[21] or lemon-squash.[22] But Mr. Kelada flashed an oriental smile at me.

"Whisky and soda or a dry Martini,[23] you have only to say the word."

From each of his hip-pockets he fished a flask and laid them on the table before me. I chose the Martini, and calling the steward he ordered a tumbler of ice and a couple of glasses.

"A very good cocktail," I said.

"Well, there are plenty more where that came from, and if you've got any friends on board, you tell them you've got a pal[24] who's got all the liquor in the world."

Mr. Kelada was chatty[25] He talked of New York and of San Francisco. He discussed plays, pictures, and politics. He was patriotic. The Union Jack is an impressive piece of drapery, but when it is flourished by a gentleman from Alexandria[26] or Beirut,[27] I cannot but feel that it loses somewhat in dignity. Mr. Kelada was familiar.[28] I do not wish to put on airs,[29] but I cannot help feeling that it is seemly[30] in a total stranger to put mister before my name when he addresses me. Mr. Kelada, doubtless to set me at my ease, used no such formality. I did not like Mr. Kelada, I had put aside the cards when he sat down, but now thinking that for this first occasion our conversation had lasted long enough, I went on with my game.

"The three on the four,"[31] said Mr. Kelada.

There is nothing more exasperating[32] when you are playing patience than to be told where to put the card you have turned up before you have had a chance to look for yourself.

"It's coming out, it's coming out,"[33] he cried. "The ten on the knave."[34]

With rage and hatred in my heart I finished. Then he seized the pack.

"Do you like card tricks?"

"No, I hate card tricks," I answered.

"Well, I'll just show you this one."

He showed me three. Then I said I would go down to the dining-room and get my seat at table.

"Oh, that's all right," he said. "I've already taken a seat for you. I thought that as we were in the same state-room[35] we might just as well sit at the same table."

I did not like Mr. Kelada.

I not only shared a cabin with him and ate three meals a day at the same table, but I could not walk round the deck without his joining me. It was impossible to snub[36] him. It never occurred to him that he was not wanted. He was certain that you were as glad to see him as he was to see you. In your own house you might have kicked him downstairs and slammed the door in his face without the suspicion dawning on him[37] that he was not a welcome visitor. He was a good mixer,[38] and in three days knew everyone on board. He ran[39] everything. He managed the sweeps,[40] conducted the auctions, collected money for prizes at the sports, got up[41] quoit[42] and golf matches, organized the concert and arranged the fancy dress ball. He was everywhere and always. He was certainly the best-hated man in the ship. We called him Mr Know-All, even to his face. He took it as a compliment. But it was at meal times that he was most intolerable. For the better part of an hour[43] then he had us at his mercy.[44] He was hearty, jovial, loquacious and argumentative. He knew everything better than anybody else, and it was an affront to his overweening vanity that you should disagree with him. He would not drop a subject, however unimportant, till he had brought you round[45] to his way of thinking. The possibility that he could be mistaken never occurred to him. He was the chap who knew. We sat at the doctor's table. Mr. Kelada would certainly have had it all his own way, for the doctor was lazy and I was frigidly indifferent, except for a man called Ramsay who sat there also. He was as dogmatic as Mr. Kelada and resented bitterly the Levantine's[46] cocksureness. The discussions they had were acrimonious[47] and interminable.

Ramsay was in the American Consular Service, and was stationed at Kobe.[48] He was on his way back to resume his post, having been on a flying[49] visit to New York to fetch his wife who had been spending a year at home. Mrs. Ramsay was a very pretty little thing, with pleasant manners and a sense of humour. The Consular Service is ill paid, and she was dressed always very simply ; but she knew how to wear her clothes. She achieved an effect of quiet distinction. I should not have paid any particular attention to her but that she possessed[50] a quality that may be common enough in women, but nowadays is not obvious in their demeanour. You could not look at her without being struck by her modesty. It shone in her like a flower in a coat.

One evening at dinner the conversation by chance drifted to the subject of pearls. There had been in the papers a good deal of talk about the culture pearls[51] which the cunning Japanese were making, and the doctor remarked that they must inevitably diminish the value of real ones. They were very good already ; they would soon be perfect. Mr. Kelada, as was his habit, rushed to the new topic. He told us all that was to be known about pearls. I do not believe Ramsay knew anything about them at all, but he could not resist the opportunity to have a fling at[52] the Levantine, and in five minutes we were in the middle of a heated argument. I had seen Mr. Kelada vehement and voluble before, but never so voluble and vehement as now. At last something that Ramsay said stung him, for he thumped the table and shouted:

"Well, I ought to know what I am talking about. I'm going to Japan just to look into[53] this Japanese pearl business. I'm in the trade and there's not a man in it who won't tell you that what I say about pearls goes.[54] I know all the best pearls in the world, and what I don't know about pearls isn't worth knowing."

Here was news for us, for Mr. Kelada, with all his loquacity, and never told anyone what his business was. We only knew vaguely that he was going to Japan on some commercial errand. He looked round the table triumphantly.

"They'll never be able to get a culture pearl that an expert like me can't tell with half an eye"[55] He pointed to a chain that Mrs. Ramsay wore. "You take my word for it, Mrs. Ramsay, that chain you're wearing will never be worth a cent less that it is now."

Mrs. Ramsay in her modest way flushed a little and slipped the chain inside her dress. Ramsay leaned forward. He gave us all a look and a smile flickered in his eyes.

"That's a pretty chain of Mrs. Ramsay's, isn't it?"

"I noticed it at once," answered Mr. Kelada. "Gee, I said to myself, those are pearls all right."[56]

"I didn't buy it myself, of course. I'd be interested to know how much you think it cost."

"Oh, in the trade[57] somewhere round fifteen thousand dollars. But if it was bought on Fifth Avenue[58] I shouldn't be surprised to hear that anything up to thirty thousand was paid for it."

Ramsay smiled grimly.

"You'll be surprised to hear that Mrs. Ramsay bought that string at a department store the day before we left New York, for eighteen dollars."

Mr. Kelada flushed.

"Rot.[59] It's not only real, but it's as fine a string for its size as I've ever seen."

"Will you bet on it? I'll bet you a hundred dollars it's imitation."

"Done."[60]

"Oh, Elmer,[61] you can't bet on a certainty,[62]" said Mrs. Ramsay. She had a little smile on her lips and her tone was gently deprecating.

"Can't I? If I get a chance of easy money like that I should be all sorts of a fool not to take it."

"But how can it be proved?" she continued. "It's only my word against Mr. Kelada's."

"Let me look at the chain, and if it's imitation I'll tell you quickly enough. I can afford to lose a hundred dollars," said Mr. Kelada.

"Take it off, dear. Let the gentleman look at it as much as he wants."

Mrs. Ramsay hesitated a moment. She put her hands to the clasp.

I can't undo it, she said. "Mr. Kelada will just have to take my word for it."

I had a sudden suspicion that something unfortunate was about to occur, but I could think of nothing to say.

Ramsay jumped up.

"I'll undo it."

He handed the chain to Mr. Kelada. The Levantine took a magnifying glass from his pocket and closely examined it. A smile of triumph spread over his smooth and swarthy[63] face. He handed back the chain. He was about to speak. Suddenly he caught sight of Mrs. Ramsay's face. It was so white that she looked as though she were about to faint. She was staring at him with wide and terrified eyes. They held a desperate appeal;[64] it was so clear that I wondered why her husband did not see it.

Mr. Kelada stopped with his mouth open. He flushed deeply. You could almost see the effort he was making over himself.[65] "I was mistaken," he said. "It's a very good imitation, but of course as soon as I looked through my glass I saw that it wasn't real. I think eighteen dollars is just about as much as the damned thing's worth."

He took out his pocket-book and from it a hundred-dollar bill. He handed it to Ramsay without a word.

"Perhaps that'll teach you not to be so cocksure another time, my young friend," said Ramsay as he took the note.

I noticed that Mr. Kelada's hands were trembling.

The story spread over the ship as stories do, and he had to put up with a good deal of chaff that evening. It was a fine joke that Mr. Know-All had been caught out.[66] But Mrs. Ramsay retired to her state-room with a headache.

Next morning I got up and began to shave. Mr. Kelada lay on his bed smoking a cigarette. Suddenly there was a small scraping sound and I saw a letter pushed under the door. I opened the door and looked out. There was nobody there. I picked up the letter and saw that it was addressed to Max Kelada. The name was written in block letters.[67] I handed it to him.

"Who's this from?" He opened it. "Oh!"

He took out of the envelope, not a letter, but a hundred-dollar note. He looked at me and again he reddened. He tore the envelope into little bits and gave them to me.

"Do you mind just throwing them out of the port-hole?"

I did as he asked, and then I looked at him with a smile.

"No one likes being made to look a perfect damned fool," he said.

"Were the pearls real?"

"If I had a pretty little wife I shouldn't let her spend a year in New York while I stayed at Kobe," said he.

At that moment I did entirely like Mr. Kelada. He reached out for[68] his pocket-book and carefully put in it the hundred-dollar note.

Footnotes

* Maugham, William Somerset(1874-1965): The novelist achieved distinction with an autobiographical novel, Of Human Bondage(1915). This is the story of Philip Carey, Who has a club foot and who attends King's School, Tercanbury ; who rejects the idea of the ministry and who studies in Heidelberg and later becomes a doctor ; who becomes obsessed with a vulgar waitress, Mildred Rogers, who goes to a bad end, etc. But the novel succeeds because of its unflinching honesty and its devastating account of loneliness, the most tragic of all human conditions. During World War I Maugham was an agent for the intelligence service, and subsequently he travelled extensively. His brilliantly successful career in fiction and drama continued and his 11 subsequent novels included The Moon and Sixpence(1919), Cakes and Ale(1930).

1) was prepared to dislike: (만나보기 전부터)~를 싫어하게 되어 있었다.
2) the ocean-going liners: 대양횡단정기객선.
3) Accommodation: room(s) for visitors or travellers as in a hotel, train, airplane and ship.
4) a cabin to yourself: 혼자 쓰는 선실
5) port-hole: opening in a ship's side for admission of light and air;현창.
6) Yokohama: 횡빈, 일본의 동경에 인접한 항도.
7) Smith or Brown: the most common British and American surnames.
8) below: carried down to the cabin.

9) **the excellent Monsieur Coty:** (the maker of) Coth toilet things ; Coty 회사의 고급화장품.

10) **brilliantine:** pomade

11) **patience:** card game for one player;solitaire.

12) **I'm, all for us English sticking together:** 영국사람들끼리 같이 있게 되는 것에는 절대 찬성이다. cf. be for : ~에 찬성하다, be against : ~에 반대하다.

13) **airily:** pompous, boastfully

14) **King George has many strange subjects:** George왕 치하에는 별 친구가 다 영국국민을 자처하는구나. King George=King Georve V.

15) **there was nothing English:** 정말 영국인이 하는 영어다운 점은 전혀 없었다.

16) **exuberant:** overflowing, abundant

17) **under a bluer sky:** somewhere south in the Mediterranean area.

18) **Prohibition:** (선내에서의) 주류판매금지.

19) **was in force:** (금지령이) 실시중이었다.

20) **bone-dry:strictly under prohibition:** 금주시간이어서 아무도 술에 취한 사람이 없었다.

21) **ginger-ale:** 생강으로 맛들인 발포성 청량음료

22) **lemon-squash:** 레몬쥬스

23) **a dry Martini:** a cocktail made of jin and vermouth;dry = unsweetened.

24) **a pal:** an intimate friend.

25) **chatty:** talkative, verbose, loquacious

26) **Alexandria:** a city in Egypt on the Mediterranean, first founded by Alexander the Great.

27) **Beirut:** the capital of Lebanon.

28) **familiar:** unduly intimate or bold ; (초면에도) 허물없이 대하는.

29) **put on airs:** behave in an unnatural way in the hope of impressing people; 거드름 피우다.

30) **seemly:** proper;correct;decent.

31) **The three on the four:** put the three on the four.

32) **exasperating:** irritating

33) **It's coming out:** 싹수가 보인다.

34) **knave:** jack.

35) **state-room:** private cabin on a steamer.

36) **snub:** 타박하다, 냉대하다.

37) **without the suspicion dawning on him that~:** without his realizing that~.

38) **He was a good mixer:** He was sociable, quick at making friends, etc.

39) **ran:** managed.

40) **the sweeps:** 돈을 모아 놓았다가 따는 사람이 다 가지는 놀이.

41) **got up:** organized.

42) **quoit:** a game in which players throw rings at a peg in the ground.

43) **For the better part of an hour:** For almost an hour.

44) **he had us at his mercy:** 그는 우리를 마음대로 했다.

45) **brought you round:** bring round = convince.

46) **Levantine:** levant = the regions on the eastern Mediterranean and the Aegean, from Greece to Egypt.

47) **acrimonious:** severe, bitter

48) **Kobe:** a city on the Southern coast of Honshu, Japan;신호(일본의 항도).

49) **flying:** 임시변통의, 갑작스레 마련한

50) **but that she possessed:** if she had not possessed.

51) **culture pearls:** artificially cultured pearls ; 양식진주.

52) **have a fling at:** 따끔하게 쏘아주다.

53) **look into:** inspect;examine.

54) **goes:** is helpful.

55) **with half an eye:** at a single glance.

56) **all right:** in every respect

57) **in the trade:** 동업자들 사이에서는. the trade = all the persons in a particular line of business.

58) **Fifth Avenue:** New York의 번화가.

59) **Rot(sl.):** Nonsense.

60) **Done:** Agreed.

61) **Elmer:** Mr. Ramsay의 given name.

62) **bet on a certainty:** 결과가 알고 걸다.

63) **swarthy:** 거무스레한, 가무잡잡한

64) **a desperate appeal:** 제발 바른 값을 말하지 말아달라는 애절한 호소.

65) **the effort he was making over himself:** 자제하려고 애쓰는 그의 노력.

66) **had been caught out:** 꼬리가 잡혔다.

67) **in block letters:** (필적을 남기지 않으려고) 활자체로 쓴.

68) **reached out for:** 팔을 뻗어 ～을 잡다.

And then there was the commuter on the train who was looking everywhere for his ticket-in his pants pocket, his jacket, his wallet. He was searching with great frenzy, much to the amusement of the other passengers, who could see that he had the ticket in his mouth. The conductor snatched the snip of paper, punched it and gave it back. When he moved on, the commuter's companion said, "I bet you feel pretty stupid sitting there looking everywhere for your ticket when it was right in your mouth all the time."

"Stupid?" replied the commuter. "I was chewing the date off."

5 The Cop and the Anthem

O. Henry[*]

On his bench in Madison Square[1)] Soapy moved uneasily. When wild geese[2)] honk high of nights,[3)] and when women without sealskin coats[4)] grow kind to their husbands, and when Soapy moves uneasily on his bench in the park, you may know that winter is near at hand.

A dead leaf fell in Soapy's lap. That was Jack Frost's[5)] card. Jack is kind to the regular denizens[6)] of Madison Square, and gives fair warning of his annual call. At the corners of four streets he hands his pasteboard[7)] to the North Wind, footman[8)] of the mansion of All Outdoors, so that the inhabitants thereof[9)] may make ready.

Soapy's mind became cognizant of the fact that the time had come for him to resolve himself into singular committee of Ways and Means[10)] to provide against the coming rigour.[11)] And therefore he moved uneasily on his bench.

The hibernatorial ambitions[12)] of Soapy were not of the highest. In them were no considerations of Mediterranean cruises, of soporific Southern skies or drifting in the Vesuvian Bay.[13)] Three months on the Island[14)] was what his soul craved. Three months of assured board and bed and congenial company, safe from Boreas[15)] and bluecoats,[16)] seemed to Soapy the essence of things desirable.

For years the hospitable Blackwell's had been his winter quarters. Just as his more fortunate fellow New Yorkers had bought their tickets to Palm Beach[17)] and the Riviera[18)] each winter, so Soapy had made his humble arrangements for his annual hegira[19)] to the Island. And now the time was come. On the previous night three Sabbath newspapers,[20] distributed beneath his coat, about his ankles and over his lap, had failed to repulse the cold as he slept on his bench near the spurting fountain in the ancient square. So the Island loomed large and timely[21] in Soapy's mind. He scorned the provisions made in the name of charity for the city's dependents. In Soapy's opinion the Law was more benign than Philanthropy. There was an endless round of[22] institutions, municipal and eleemosynary, on which he might set out and receive lodging and food accordant with the simple life. But to one[23] of Soapy's proud spirit the gifts of charity are encumbered.[24] If not in coin you must pay in humiliation of spirit for every benefit received at the hands[25] of philanthropy. As Caesar had his Brutus, every bed of charity must have its toll of a bath,[26] every loaf of bread[27] its compensation of a private and personal inquisition. Wherefore it is better to be a guest of the law, which though conducted by rules, does not meddle unduly with[28] a gentleman's private affairs.

Soapy, having decided to go to the Island, at once set about accomplishing his desire. There were many easy ways of doing this. The pleasantest was to dine luxuriously at some expensive restaurant ; and then, after declaring insolvency, be handed over[29] quietly and without uproar to a policeman. An accommodating magistrate would do the rest.

Soapy left his bench and strolled out of the square and across the level sea of asphalt, where Broadway and Fifty Avenue flow together. Up Broadway he turned, and halted at a glittering café, where are gathered together nightly the choicest products of the grape, the silkworm and the protoplasm.[30]

Soapy had confidence in himself from the lowest button of his vest upward. He was shaven, and his coat was decent and his neat black, ready-tied four-in-hand[31] had been presented to him by a lady missionary on Thanksgiving Day. If he could reach a table in the restaurant unsuspected success would be his. The portion of him that would show above the table would raise no doubt in the waiter's mind. A roasted mallard duck, thought Soapy, would be about the thing[32]—with a bottle of Chablis,[33] and then Camembert,[34] a demitasse[35] and a cigar. One dollar for the cigar would be enough. The total would not be so high as to call forth any supreme manifestation of revenge from the café management ; and yet the meat would leave him filled and happy for the journey to his winter refuge.

But as Soapy set foot inside the restaurant door the head waiter's eye fell upon his frayed trousers and decadent shoes. Strong and ready hands turned him about and conveyed him in silence and haste to the sidewalk and averted the ignoble fate of the menaced mallard.

Soapy turned off Broadway. It seemed that his route to the coveted Island was not to be an epicurean one. Some other way of entering limbo[36] must be thought of.

At a corner of Sixth Avenue electric lights and cunningly displayed wares behind plate-glass made a shop window conspicuous. Soapy took a cobble-stone and dashed it through the glass. People came running round the corner, a policeman in the lead.[37] Soapy stood still, with his hands in his pockets, and smiled at the sight of brass buttons.

"Where's the man that done that?"[38] inquired the officer excitedly.

"Don't you figure out[39] that I might have had something to do with it?" said Soapy, not without sarcasm,[40] but friendly, as one greets good fortune.

The policeman's mind refused to accept Soapy even as a clue. Men who smash windows do not remain to parley with[41] the law's minions. They take to their heels.[42] The policeman saw a man half-way down the block runnung to catch a car. With drawn club he joined in the pursuit. Soapy, with disgust in his heart, loafed along, twice unsuccessful.

On the opposite side of the street was a restaurant of no great pretensions.[43] It catered to large appetites and modest purses. Its crockery and atmosphere were thick ; its soup and napery[44] thin. Into this place Soapy took his accusive shoes and telltale trousers without challenge. At a table he sat and consumed beefsteak, flapjacks,[45] doughnuts and pie. And then to the waiter he betrayed the fact that the minutest coin and himself were strangers.

"Now, get busy[46] and call a cop," said Soapy, "And don't keep a gentleman waiting."

"No cop for you," said the waiter, with a voice like butter cakes and an eye like the cherry in a Manhattan cocktail. "Hey, Con!"

Neatly upon his left ear on the callous pavement two waiters pitched Soapy. He arose, joint by joint, as a carpenter's rule opens, and beat the dust from his clothes. Arrest seemed but a rosy dream. The Island seemed very far away. A policeman who stood before a drugstore two doors away laughed and walked down the street.

Five blocks Soapy travelled before his courage permitted him to woo[47] capture again. This time the opportunity presented what he fatuously termed to himself a "cinch."[48] A young woman of a modest and pleasing guise[49] was standing before a show window gazing with sprightly[50] interest at its display of shaving mugs and inkstands, and two yards from the window a large policeman of severe demeanour leaned against a water plug.

It was Soapy's design to assume the role of the despicable and execrated "masher."[51] The refined and elegant appearance of his victim and the contiguity of the conscientious cop encouraged him to believe that he would soon feel the pleasant official clutch upon his arm[52] that would ensure his winter quarters on the tight little isle.

Soapy straightened the lady missionary's readymade tie, dragged his shrinking cuffs into the open, set his hat at a killing cant[53] and sidled toward the young woman. He made eyes at[54] her, was taken with[55] sudden coughs and "hems," smiled, smirked and went brazenly through the impudent and contemptible litany[56] of the "masher." With half an eye Soapy saw that the policeman was watching him fixedly. The young woman moved away a few steps, and again bestowed her absorbed attention upon the shaving mugs. Soapy followed, boldly stepping to her side, raised his hat and said:

"Ah, there. Bedelia! Don't you want to come and play in my yard?"[57]

The policeman was still looking. The persecuted young woman had but to[58] beckon a finger and Soapy would be practically en route[59] for his insular haven. Already he imagined he could feel the cosy warmth of the station-house.[60] The young woman faced him and, stretching out a hand, caught Soapy's coat sleeve.

"Sure, Mike," she said joyfully, "if you'll blow[61] me to a pail of suds.[62] I'd have spoken to you sooner but the cop was watching."

With the young woman playing the clinging ivy to his oak[63] Soapy walked past the policeman overcome with gloom. He seemed doomed to liberty.[64]

At the next corner he shook off his companion and ran. He halted in the district where by night are found the lightest streets, hearts, vows and librettos.[65] Women in furs and men in greatcoats moved gaily in the wintry air. A sudden fear seized Soapy that[66] some dreadful enchantment had rendered him immune to arrest. The thought brought a little of panic upon it, and when he came upon another policeman lounging grandly in front of a transplendent[67] theatre he caught at the immediate straw of[68] "disorderly conduct."[69]

On the sidewalk Soapy began to yell drunken gibberish at the top of his harsh voice. He danced, howled, raved and otherwise disturbed the welkin.[70]

The policeman twirled his club, turned his back to Soapy and remarked to a citizen.

"'Tis[71] one of them[72] Yale lads celebratin' the goose egg[73] they give to the Hartford College. Noisy but no harm. We've instructions to leave them be."

Disconsolate, Soapy ceased his unavailing racket.[74] Would never a policeman lay hands on him? In his fancy the Island seemed an unattainable Arcadia.[75] He buttoned his thin coat against the chilling wind.

In a cigar store he saw a well-dressed man lighting a cigar at a swinging light. His silk umbrella he had set by the door on entering. Soapy stepped inside, secured the umbrella and sauntered off[76] with it slowly. The man at the cigar light followed hastily.

"My umbrella," he said, sternly.

"Oh, is it?" sneered Soapy, adding insult to petit larceny.[77] "Well, why don't you call a policeman? I took it. Your umbrella! Why don't you call a cop? There stands one on the corner."

The umbrella owner slowed his steps. Soapy did like-wise, with a presentiment that luck would again run against him. The policeman looked at the two curiously.

"Of course," said the umbrella man—"that is—well, you know how these mistakes occur—I—if it's your umbrella I hope you'll excuse me—I picked it up this morning in a restaurant—If you recognize it as yours, why—I hope you'll—"

"Of course it's mine," said Soapy, viciously.

The ex-umbrella man retreated. The policeman hurried to assist a tall blonde[78] in an opera cloak across the street in front of street car that was approaching two blocks away.

Soapy walked eastward through a street damaged by improvements.[79] He hurled the umbrella wrathfully into an excavation. He muttered against the men who wear helmets and carry clubs. Because he wanted to fall into their clutches, they seemed to regard him as a king who could do no wrong.

At length Soapy reached one of the avenues to the east where the glitter and turmoil was but faint. He set his face down this toward Madison Square, for the homing instinct survives even when the home is a park bench.

But on an unusually quiet corner Soapy came to a stand-still.

Here was an old church, quaint and rambling[80] and gabled.[81] Through one violet-stained window a soft light glowed, where, no doubt the organist loitered over the keys, making sure of his mastery of the coming Sabbath anthem. For there drifted out to Soapy's ears sweet music that caught and held him transfixed[82] against the convolutions[83] of the iron fence.

The moon was above, lustrous and serene ; vehicles and pedestrians were few ; sparrows twittered sleepily in the eaves[84]—for a little while the scene might have been a country churchyard. And the anthem that the organist played cemented Soapy to the iron fence, for he had known it well in the days when his life contained such things as mothers and roses and ambitions and friends and immaculate[85] thoughts and collars.

The conjunction of Soapy's receptive state of mind and the influences about the old church wrought a sudden and wonderful change in his soul. He viewed with swift horror the pit into which he had tumbled, the degraded days, unworthy desires, dead hopes, wrecked faculties and base motives that made up his existence.

And also in a moment his heart responded thrillingly to this novel mood. An instantaneous and strong impulse moved him to battle with his desperate fate. He would pull himself out of the mire ; he would make a man of himself again ; he would conquer the evil that had taken possession of him. There was time ; he was comparatively young yet ; he would resurrect his old eager ambitions and pursue them without faltering. Those solemn but sweet organ notes had set up a revolution in him. Tomorrow he would go into the roaring downtown district and find work. A fur importer had once offered him a place as driver. He would find him tomorrow and ask for the position.

He would be somebody[86] in the world. He would—

Soapy felt a hand laid on his arm. He looked quickly around into the broad face of a policeman.

"What are you doin' here?" asked the officer.

"Nothin'," said Soapy.

"Then come along," said the policeman.

"Three months on the Island," said the Magistrate in the Police Court the next morning.

*O. Henry : (1862-1910); real name, William Sidney Portere; 미국 단편작가.

1) Madison Square: New York 시 중심지의 광장.

2) wild geese: 기러기. geese = goose(거위)의 pl.

3) of nights: by night ; at night;밤에는.

4) sealskin coats: (부인용) 물개 가죽 외투.

5) Jack Frost: frost personified.

6) denizens: inhabitants. 7) pasteboard:(속)명함.

8) footman: man−servant who admits visitors, waits at table, etc.

9) inhabitants thereof: inhabitants of it(the mansion.)

10) resolve himself into···Means: 자기 스스로가 일인대책위원회의 위원이 된다.

11) provide against the coming rigour: 다가올 혹한에 대비하다.

12) hibernatorial ambitions: 겨울을 춥지 않게 지나려는 여러 가지 생각.

13) the Vesuvian Bay: 이탈리앙 남부 나폴리 맞은 편에 있는 Vesuvius 화산 주변의 만.

14) the Island: Welfare Island ; until 1921 known as Blackwells Island ; Island in East river, New York City ; municipal hospital, and formerly a pneal institution.

15) Boreas: (희신) 북풍의 신. 16) bluecoats : (미) 순경.

17) Palm Beach: 대서양으로 면한 Florida주 해안의 피한지.

18) the Riviera: 프랑스의 Nice에서 이탈리아의 La Slpezia에 이르는 해안지대 ; 경치좋은 피한지.

19) hegira: 도피 ; Muhammad's flight from Mecca to Medina(A. D. 622).

20) Sabbath newspapers: (교회에서 공짜로 얻어볼 수 있는) 일요신문.

21) loomed large and timely: appeared to be important and opportune.

22) round of: number of. 23) one : a man.

24) **encumbered**: cumbersome ; burdensome ; 마음에 걸리는(부담이 되는).

25) **received at the hands**: reveived from the peersons.

26) **its toll of a bath**: 침대에서 자려면 목욕을 꼭 해야 하는 것이 세금을 내는 것과 같다는 뜻.

27) **bread** : 다음에 "must have"를 넣어서 해석해 볼 것.

28) **meddle unduly with**: 과도하게 ~을 간섭하다.

29) **be handed over**: to dine의 to에 걸린다.

30) **protoplasm**: colourless, jelly-like substance which is material basis of life in animals and plants; 원형질(생). 여기서 products of the protoplasm은 인간들을 말한다.

31) **four-in-hand**: (보통매는) neck-tie. 32) about the thing : 적당한.

33) **Chablis[ʃæbli]**: (프랑스 Chablis 원산) 백포도주.

34) **Camembert[kɑ:məbə]**: 프랑스산 치즈의 일종.

35) **demitasse[dimi-tʌs]**: (F) black coffee. 36) limbo : prison.

37) **a policeman in the lead**: with a policeman at the head.

38) **the man that done that**: the man who has done that.

39) **Don't you figure out…?**: Don't you image…?

40) **not without sarcasm**: 좀 빈정대며.

41) **parley with**: talk with. 42) take to their heels : run away.

43) **of no great pretensions**: 그다지 훌륭하지 않은.

44) **napery**: table linen(tablecloths and napkins).

45) **flapjack**: griddle cake ; hotcake ; pancake.

46) **get busy**: take an action. 47) woo : try to win.

48) **cinch**: (미·속) 쉬운 일, 거저먹기 ; something easy and sure.

49) **guise**: (old use) style of dress. 50) sprightly ; (adj.) lively ; 활발한.

51) **execrated "masher"**: hated "lady-killer." ; 사회에서 미움받는 난봉꾼.

52) **official clutch upon his arm**: arrest.

53) **at a killing cant**: (보면) 절로 웃음이 (터져)나올만큼 비스듬이. killing = amusing, comical;cant = sloping or sideways position ; tilt (경사)

54) **made eyes at**: ~에게 추파를 던졌다.

55) **was taken with**: 시작했다.

56) **litany**: 여기서는 난봉꾼이 여자를 유혹할 때 쓰는 판에 박은 듯한 말, 즉 유혹의 정석.

57) **play in my yard**: play with me.

58) **had but to: had only to**: ~하기만 하면 되었다.

59) **en route**: (F.) on the way. 60) station-house : (U. S. A.) police station.

61) **blow**: (sl.) spend(money) recklessly or extravagantly ; 한턱 내다.

62) **a pail lof suds**: a glass of beer. suds = froth, mass of tiny bubblels, on sopy water (거품).

63) **playing the clinging ivy to his oak**: 참나무를 휘감은 담쟁이 같이 그에게 매달리는 ; (그를 참나무, 그 여자를 담쟁이에 비유한 것.)

64) doomed to liberty: 다음에 나오는 "immune to arrest"와 같음.

65) hearts, vows, librettos: 애인들, 사랑의 속삭임, 연극들.

66) that some…: that 이하는 fear와 동격.

67) transplendent: 백광 찬란한.

68) of는 동격의 "of." Cf. A drowing man will catch at a straw.

69) "disorderly conduct": 풍기 문란죄. 70) the welkin : (시) 하늘(sky).

71) Tis: (시·방) It is의 단축형. 72) them : (방) those.

73) goose egg: cuk's egg ; (경) 영점.

74) racket: 소동, 난동. 75) Arcadia : utopia.

76) saunter off: 산책하다. 77) petit larceny : small theft.

78) blonde: cf. blond(남)

79) a street damaged by improvements: 도로공사로 파 헤쳐진 거리.

80) rambling: (esp. of buildings, streets, towns), extending in various directions irregularly, as if built without planning ; 들쑥 날쑥한, 요철의.

81) gabled: (건) 박풍이 달린. gable = three-cornered part of an outside wall between sloping roofs.

82) transfixed: 꼼짝 못하게 하다. 83) convolutions : 나선, 모선

84) eaves: 처마, 차양. 85) immaculate : 청순한, 순결한

86) somebody: a person of some importance.

"You will have exactly two hours," said the professor as he handed out examination papers to a roomful lof students. "Under no circumstances will I accept a paper given to me after the deadline has passed." Two hours later he broke the silence. "Time is up," he said. But one student continued to work furiously.

The professor war glaring out from behind the pile of exams when the tardy student approached him, almost 15minutes later, with his exam clutched behind his back. When the professor refused to accept it, the student drew himself up to full stature and asked, "Professor, do you know who I am?"

"No," said the professor.

"Terrific," replied the student, and he stuffed his paper into the middle of the pile.

6 Love Is a Fallacy

Max Shulman[*]

Cool was I and logical. Keen, calculating, perspicacious,[1)] acute and astute—I was all of these. My brain was as powerful as a dynamo, as precise as a chemist's scales, as penetrating as a scalpel. And—think of it!—I was only eighteen.

It is not often that one so young has such a giant intellect. Take, for example, Petey Bellows, my roommate at the university. Same age, same background, but dumb as an ox. A nice enough fellow, you understand, but nothing upstairs.[2)] Emotional type. Unstable. Impressionable. Worst of all, a faddist. Fads, I submit, are the very negative of reason. To be swept up in every new craze that comes along, to surrender yourself to idiocy just because everybody else is doing it—this, to me, is acme of mindlessness. Not however, to Petey.

One afternoon I found Petey lying on his bed with an expression of such distress on his face that I immediately diagnosed appendicitis.[3)] "Don't move," I said. "Don't take a laxative.[4)] I'll get a doctor."

"Raccoon," he mumbled thickly.

"Raccoon?" I said, pausing in my flight.

"I want a raccoon coat," he wailed.

I perceived that his trouble was not physical, but mental. "Why do you want a raccoon coat?"

"I should have known it," he cried, pounding his temples. "I should have known they'd[5)] come back when the Charleston[6)] came back. Like a fool I spent all my money for textbooks, and I can't get a raccoon coat."

"Can you mean," I said incredulously, "that people are actually wearing raccoon coats again?"

"All the Big Men on Campus are wearing them. Where've you been?"

"In the library," I said, naming a place not frequented by Big Men on Campus.

He leaped from the bed and paced the room. "I've got to have a raccoon coat," he said passionately. "I've got to!"

"Petey, why? Look at it rationally. Raccoon coats are unsanitary. They shed.[7] They smell bad. They weigh too much. They're unsightly. They—"

"You don't understand," he interrupted impatiently. "It's the thing to do. Don't you want to be in the swim?"[8]

"No," I said, truthfully.

"Well, I do," he declared, "I'd give anything for a raccoon coat. Anything!"

My brain, that precision instrument, slipped into high gear. "Anything," he affirmed in ringing tones.

I stroked my chin thoughtfully. It so happened that I knew where to get my hands on a raccoon coat. My father had had one in his undergraduate days ; it lay now in a trunk in the attic back home. It also happened that Petey had something I wanted. He didn't have it exactly, but at least he had first right on it. I refer to his girl, Polly Espy.

I had long coveted Polly Eapy. Let me emphasize that my desire for this young woman was not emotional in nature. She was, to be sure, a girl who excited the emotions, but I was not one to let my heart rule my head. I wanted Polly for a shrewdly calculated, entirely cerebral[9] reason.

I was a freshman in law school. In a few years I would be out in practice. I was well aware of the importance of the right kind of wife in furthering a lawyer's career. The successful lawyers I had observed were, almost without exception, married to beautiful, gracious, intelligent woman. With one omission. Polly fitted these specifications perfectly.

Beautiful she was. She was not yet of pin-up proportions[10] but I felt sure that time would supply the lack. She already had the makings.[11]

Gracious she was. By gracious I mean full of graces. She had an erectness of carriage,[12] an ease of bearing, a poise that clearly indicated the best of breeding. At table her manners were exquisite. I had seen her at the Kozy Kampus Korner[13] eating the specialty[14] of the house-a sandwich that contained scraps of pot roast, gravy, chopped nuts, and a dipper of sauerkraut-without even getting her fingers moist.

Intelligent she was not. In fact, she veered in the opposite direction. But I believed that under my guidance she would smarten up. At any rate, it was worth a try. It is, after all, easier to make a beautiful dumb girl smart than to make an ugly smart girl beautiful.

"Petey," I said, "are you in love with Polly Espy?"

"I think she's a keen kid," he replied, "but I don't know if you'd call it love. Why?"

"Do you," I asked, "have any kind of formal arrangement with her? I mean are you going steady or anything like that?"

"No. We see each other quite a bit, but we both have other dates. Why?"

"Is there," I asked, "any other man for whom she has a particular fondness?"

"Not that I know of. Why?"

I nodded with satisfaction. "In other words, if you were out of the picture, the field would be open. Is that right?"

"I guess so. What are you getting at?"

"Nothing, nothing," I said innocently, and took my suitcase out of the closet.

"Where you going?" asked Petey.

"Home for the week end." I threw a few things into the bag.

"Listen," he said, clutching my arm eagerly, "while you're home, you couldn't get some money from your old man, could you,[15] and lend it to me so I can buy a raccoon coat?"

"I may do better than that," I said with a mysterious wink and closed my bag and left.

"Look," I said to Petey when I got back Monday morning. I threw open the suitcase and revealed the huge, hairy object that my father had worn in 1925.

"Holy Toledo!" said Petey reverently. He plunged his hands into the raccoon coat and then his face. "Holy Toledo!" he repeated fifteen or twenty times.

"Would you like it?" I asked.

"Oh yes!" he cried, clutching the greasy pelt to him. Then a canny look came into his eyes. "What do you want for it?"

"Your girl," I said, mincing no words.[16]

"Polly?" he said in a horrified whisper. "You want Polly?"

"That's right."

He flung the coat from him. "Never," he said stoutly.

I shrugged. "Okey. If you don't want to be in the swim, I guess it's your business."

I sat down in a chair and pretended to read a book, but out of the corner of my eye I kept watching Petey. He was a torn man. First he looked at the coat with the expression of a waif[17] at a bakery window. Then he turned away and set his jaw resolutely. Then he looked back at the coat, with even more longing in his face. Then he turned away, but with not so much resolution this time. Back and forth his head swiveled, desire waxing, resolution waning. Finally he didn't turn away at all ; he just stood and stared with mad lust at the coat.

"It isn't as though I was in love with Polly," he said thickly. "Or going steady or anything like that."

"That's right," I murmured.

"What's Polly to me, or me to Polly?"

"Not a thing," said I.

"It's just been a casual kick[18]—just a few laughs, that's all"

"Try on the coat," said I.

He complied. The coat bunched high over his ears and dropped all the way down to his shoe tops. He looked like a mound of dead raccoons. "Fits fine," he said happily.

I rose from my chair. "Is it a deal?" I asked, extending my hand.

He swallowed. "It's a deal." he said and shook my hand.

I had my first date with Polly the following evening. This was in the nature of a survey ; I wanted to find out just how much work I had to do to get her mind up to the standard I required. I took her first to dinner. "Gee, that was a delicious dinner," she said as we left the restaurant. Then I took her to a movie. "Gee, that was a marvy[19] movie," she said as we left the theater. And then I took her home. "Gee, I had a sensaysh time," she said as she bade me good night.

I went back to my room with a heavy heart. I had gravely underestimated the size of my task. This girl's lack of information was terrifying. Nor would it be enough merely to supply her with information. First she had to be taught to think. This loomed as a project of no small dimensions, and at first I was tempted to give her back to Petey. But then I got to thinking about her abundant physical charms and about the way she entered a room and the way she handled a knife and fork, and I decided to make an effort.

I went about it, as in all things, systematically. I gave her a course in logic.

It happened that I, as a law student, was taking a course in logic myself so I had all the facts at my finger tips. "Polly," I said to her when I picked her up in our next date, "tonight we are going over to the Knoll and talk."

"Oo, terrif,"[20] she replied. One thing I will say for this girl: you would go far to find another so agreeable.

We went to the Knoll, the campus trysting place,[21] and we sat down under an old oak, and she looked at me expectantly. "What are we going to talk about?" she asked.

"Logic," I said, clearing my throat, "is the science of thinking. Before we can think correctly, we must first learn to recognize the common fallacies of logic. These we will take up tonight."

"Wow-dow!" she cried, clapping her hands delightedly.

I winced, but went bravely on. "First let us examine the fallacy called Dicto Simpliciter."[22]

"By all means," she urged, batting her lashes eagerly.

"Dicto Simpliciter means an argument based on an unqualified generalization. For example : Exercise is good. Therefore everybody should exercise."

"I agree," said Polly earnestly. "I mean exercise is wonderful. I mean it builds the body and everything."

"Polly," I said gently, "the argument is a fallacy. Exercise is good is an unqualified generalization. For instance, if you have heart disease, exercise is bad, not good. Many people are ordered by their doctors not to exercise. You must qualify the generalization. You must say exercise is usually good, or exercise is good for most people. Otherwise you have committed a Dicto Simpliciter. Do you see?"

"No," she confessed. "But this is marvy. Do more! Do more!"

"It will be better if you stop tugging at my sleeve," I told her, and when she desisted,[23] I continued. "Next we take up a fallacy called Hasty Generalization. Listen carefully : You can't speak French. I can't speak French. Petey Bellows can't speak French. I must therefore conclude that nobody at the University of Minnesota can speak French."

"Really?" said Polly, amazed. "Nobody?"

I hid my exasperation. "Polly, it's a fallacy. The generalization is reached too hastily. There are too few instances to support such a conclusion."

"Know any more fallacies?" she asked breathlessly "This is more fun than dancing even."

I fought off a wave of despair. I was getting nowhere with this girl, absolutely nowhere. Still, I am nothing if not persistent. I continued. "Next comes Post Hoc.[24] Listen to this : Let's not take Bill on our picnic. Every time we take him out with us, it rains."

"I know somebody just like that," she exclaimed. "A girl back home—Eula Becker, her name is. It never fails. Every single time we take her on a picnic —"

"Polly," I said sharply, "it's a fallacy. Eula Becker doesn't cause the rain. She has no connection with the rain. You are guilty of Post Hoc if you blame Eula Becker."

"I'll never do it again," she promised contritely. "Are you mad at me?"

I sighed. "No, Polly, I'm not mad."

"Then tell me some more fallacies."

"All right. Let's try Contradictory Premises."

"Yes, let's," she chirped, blinking her eyes happily. I frowned but plunged ahead. "Here's an example of Contradictory Premises : If God can do anything, can He make a stone so heavy that He won't be able to lift it?"

"Of course," she replied promptly.

"But if He can do anything He can lift the stone," I pointed out.

"Yeah," she said thoughtfully. "Well, then I guess He can't make the stone."

"But He can do anything," I reminded her.

She scratched her pretty, empty head. "I'm all confused," she admitted.

"Of course you are. Because when the premises of an argument contradict each other, there can be no argument. If there is an irresistable force, there can be no immovable object. If there is an immovable object, there can be no irresistible force. Get it?"

"Tell me some more of this keen stuff," she said eagerly.

I consulted my watch. "I think we'd better call it a night.[25] I'll take you home now, and you go over all the things you've learned. We'll have another session tomorrow night."

I deposited her at girls' dormitory, where she assured me that she had had perfectly terrif evening, and I went glumly home to my room. Petey lay snoring in his bed, the raccoon coat huddled like a great hairy beast at his feet. For a moment I considered waking him and telling him that he could have his girl back. It seemed clear my project was doomed to failure. The girl simply had a logicproof head.

But then I reconsidered. I had wasted one evening ; I might as well waste another. Who knew? Maybe somewhere in the extinct crater of her mind a few embers still smoldered. Maybe somehow I could fan them into a flame. Admittedly it was not a prospect fraught with[26] hope, but I decided to give it one more try.

Seated under the oak the next evening I said, "Our first fallacy tonight is called Ad Misericordiam."[27]

She quivered with delight.

"Listen closely," I said. "A man applies for a job. When the boss asks him what his qualifications are, he replies that he has a wife and six children at home, the wife is a helpless cripple, the children have nothing to eat, no clothes to wear, no shoes on their feet, there are no beds in the house, no coal in the cellar, and winter is coming."

A tear rolled down each of Polly's pink cheeks. "Oh, this is awful, awful," she sobbed.

"Yes, it's awful," I agreed, "but it's no argument. The man never answered the boss's question about his qualifications. Instead he appeals to boss's sympathy. He committed the fallacy of Ad Misericordiam. Do you understand?"

"Have you got a handkerchief?" she blubbered.

I handed her a handkerchief and tried to keep from screaming while she wiped her eyes. "Next," I said in a carefully controlled tone, "We will discuss False Analogy. Here is an example : Students should be allowed to look at their textbooks during examinations. After all, surgeons have X-rays to guide them during an operation, lawyers have beliefs to guide them during a trial, carpenters have blueprints to guide them when they are building a house. Why, then, shouldn't students be allowed to look at their textbooks during an examination?"

"There now," she said enthusiastically, "is the most marvy idea I've heard in years."

"Polly," I said testily, "the argument is all wrong. Doctors, lawyers, and carpenters arent's taking a test to see how much they have learned, but students are. The situations are altogether different, and you can't make an analogy between them."

"I still think it's good idea," said Polly.

"Nuts,"[28] I muttered. Doggedly I pressed on. "Next we'll try Hypothesis Contrary to Fact."

"Sounds yummy,"[29] was Polly's reaction.

"Listen : If Madame Curie had not happened to leave a photographic plate in a drawer with a chunk of pitchblende, the world today would not know about radium."

"True, true," said Polly, nodding her head. "Did you see the movie? Oh, it just knocked me out. That Walter Pidgeon is so dreamy. I mean he fractures me."

"If you can forget Mr. Pidgeon for a moment," I said coldly, "I would like to point out that the statement is a fallacy. Maybe Madame Curie would have discovered radium at some later date. Maybe somebody else would have discovered it. Maybe any number of things would have happened. You can't start with a hypothesis that is not true and then draw any supportable conclusions from it."

"They ought to put Walter Pidgeon in more pictures," said Polly. "I hardly ever see him any more."

One more chance, I decided. But just one more. There is a limit to what flesh and blood can bear. "The next fallacy is called Poisoning the Well."

"How cute!" she gurgled.

"Two men are having a debate. The first one gets up and says, 'My opponent is a notorious liar. You can't believe a word that he is going to say⋯.' Now, Polly, think. Think hard. What's wrong?"

I watched her closely as she knit her creamy brow in concentration. Suddenly a glimmer of intelligence—the first I had seen—came into her eyes. "It's not fair," she said with indignation. "It's not a bit fair. What chance has the second man got if the first man calls him a liar before he even begins talking?"

"Right!" I cried exultantly. "One hundred per cent right. It's not fair. The first man has poisoned the well before anybody could drink from it. He has hamstrung[30] his opponent before he could even start⋯ Polly, I'm proud of you."

"Pshaw," she murmured, blushing with pleasure.

"You see, my dear, these things aren't so hard. All you have to do is concentrate. Think-examine-evaluate. Come now, let's review everything we have learned."

"Fire away,"[31] she said with an airy wave of her hand.

Heartened by the knowledge that Polly was not altogether a cretin, I began a long, patient review of all I had told her. Over and over and over again I cited instances, pointed out flaws, kept hammering away without letup. It was like digging a tunnel. At first everything was work, sweat, and darkness. I had no idea when I would reach the light, or even if I would. But I persisted. I pounded and clawed and scraped, and finally I was rewarded. I saw a chink of light.[32] And then the chink got bigger, and the sun came pouring in and all was bright.

Five grueling nights this took, but it was worth it. I had made a logician out of Polly ; I had taught her to think. My job was done. She was worthy of me at last. She was a fit wife for me, a proper hostess for my many mansions, a suitable mother for my wellheeled children.

It must not be thought that I was without love for this girl. Quite the contrary. Just as Pygmalion[33] loved the perfect woman he had fashioned, so I loved mine. I decided to acquaint here with my feelings at our very next meeting. The time had come to change our relationship from academic to romantic.

"Polly," I said when next we sat beneath our oak, "tonight we will not discuss fallacies."

"Aw, gee," she said, disappointed.

"My dear," I said, favoring her with a smile, "we have now spent five evenings together. We have gotten along splendidly. It is clear that we are well matched."

"Hasty Generalization," she repeated. "How can you say that we are well matched on the basis of only five dates?"

I chuckled with amusement. The dear child had learned her lessons well. "My dear," I said, patting her hand in a tolerant manner, "five dates is plenty. After all, you don't have to eat a whole cake to know that it's good."

"False Analogy," said Polly promptly. "I'm not a cake. I'm a girl."

I chuckled with somewhat less amusement. The dear child had learned her lessons perhaps too well. I decided to change tactics. Obviously, the best approach was a simple, strong, direct declaration of love. I paused for a moment while my massive brain chose the proper words. Then I began:

"Polly, I love you. You are the whole world to me, and the moon and the stars and the constellations[34] of outer space. Please, my darling, say that you will go steady with me, for if you will not, life will be meaningless. I will languish. I will refuse my meals. I will wander the face of the earth, a shambling, hollow-eyed hulk."

There, I thought, folding my arms, that ought to do it.

"Ad Misericordiam," said Polly.

I ground my teeth. I was not Pygmalion ; I was Frankenstein,[35] and my monster had me by the throat. Frantically I fought back the tide of panic surging through me. At all costs I had to keep cool.

"Well, Polly," I said, forcing a smile, "you certainly have learned your fallacies,"

"You're darn[36] right," she said with a vigorous nod.

"And who taught them to you, Polly?"

"You did."

"That's right. So you do owe me something, don't you, my dear? If I hadn't come along you never would have learned about fallacies."

"Hypothesis Contrary to Fact," she said instantly.

I dashed perspiration[37] from my brow. "Polly," I croaked, "you mustn't take all these things so literally. I mean this is just classroom stuff. You know that the things you learn in school don't have anything to do with life."

"Dicto Simpliciter," she said, wagging her finger at me playfully.

That did it. I leaped to my feet, bellowing like a bull. "Will you or will you not go steady with me?"

"I will not," she replied.

"Why not?" I demanded.

"Because this afternoon I promised Petey Bellows that I would go steady with him."

I reeled back,[38] overcome with the infamy of it. After he promised, after he made a deal, after he shook my hand! "The rat!" I shrieked, kicking up great chunks of turf. "You can't go with him, Polly. He's a liar. He's a cheat. He's a rat."

"Poisoning the Well," said Polly, "and stop shouting. I think shouting must be a fallacy too."

With an immense effort of will, I modulated my voice. "All right," I said. "You're a logician. Let's look at this thing logically. How could you choose Petey Bellows over me? Look at me—a brilliant student, a tremendous intellectual, a man with an assured future. Look at Petey—a knothead, a jitterbug,[39] a guy who'll never know where his next meal is coming from. Can you give me one logical reason why you should go steady with Petey Bellows?"

"I certainly can," declared Polly. "He's got a raccoon coat."

* Max Shulman: (1919~)미국작가.

1) perespicacious: clever

2) nothing upstairs: no brains.

3) appendicitis: 맹장염

4) laxative: 완하제

5) they: raccoon coats.

6) the Charleston: a type of lively dance, in 4/4 time.

7) shed: 털이 빠지다

8) be in the swim: 시류나 유행을 따르다.

9) cerebral: 대뇌의, 이지적인

10) pin-up proportions: 팔등신 미인

11) have the makings: 소질이 있다.

12) carriage: 몸가짐

13) the Kozy Kampus Korner: the cozy campus corner. 구내 식당같은 곳.

14) specialty: 특식

15) you couldn't get some money from your old man, could you:you could get some money from your old man, couldn't you?

16) mincing no words: 또는 직업적으로 말하다.

17) waif: 부랑아(ex. waifs and strays)

18) kick: excitement ; thrill.

19) marvy: marvelous.

20) terrif: terrific ; thrilling.

21) trysting place: 밀회장소

22) Dicto Simpliciter: arguing from some accidental fact as if it were essential.

23) desisted: 그만두다, 중지하다.

24) Post Hoc: (post hoc, ergo proper hoc) happening after this, therefore happening because of it.

25) call it a night: 끝내다.

26) fraught with: ~으로 가득찬

27) Ad Misericordiam: an appeal to mercy or pity.

28) nuts: 제기랄, 바보같은 소리.

29) yummy: (미속) 기분 좋은, 즐거운.

30) hamstrung: 불구로 만들다, 못쓰게 하다.

31) fire away: 시작하다.

32) **a chink of light:** 한줄기 불빛
33) **Pygmalion:** a king of Cyprus in Greek legend who carved the statue that turned into the beautiful maiden Galatea.
34) **constellations:** 성차
35) **Frankenstein:** the name of the scientist who created a monster in Mary Shelley's novel.
36) **darn:** damn
37) **perspiration:** 땀
38) **reeled back:** 비틀거리다. 휘청거리다.
39) **jitterbug:** 춤쟁이

When Goliath came against Israelites, the soldiers all thought, "He's so big we can never kill him." David looked at the same giant and thought, "He's so big I can't miss."

PART 4

• • •

문제 연습

Through the Eyes of Children

Teletubbie, which is becoming more and more popular these days among small students, is a new kids program which targets under five years old. Compared with other children's programs which used to gain about 7% of the audience share, this program recorded an 18% program rating, which is the highest among kids' program. Catching up with other programs in just one month from Oct.12 of last year, it is enough to attract public attention. There is some evidence which supports the great popularity of the Teletubbie. When its broadcasting time changed from 8:15 a.m. to 9:00 a.m., phone calls poured in from the audience raising objection to the change. They said that their children would not go to kindergarten because the time coincided with the Teletubbie program. Then what makes this program so popular? The answer is not simple but very complex. The program focuses on infants at the earliest level of language acquisition. All the elements and the environment set up in the program were developed based on the result of elaborate and thorough studies of very young children. The characters' external abnormal appearance - short legs and arms, big head, and a big rump covered with a diaper - mirrors the real bodies of infants themselves. The elaborate and exhaustive marketing plan of BBC has played an important role in its enormous popularity. The fact that the target audience of this program is children under five years old worked as another big factor because they are too young to perceive cultural differences between nations. The BBC has focused on this point, and has been totally successful in that sense as the show is broadcast in 27 countries including Korea.

1. Which of the following is correct?

(A) The program is provided from 8:15 a.m. to 9:00 a.m.

(B) Kids' program usually records an 18% program rating.

(C) The program is a special program of language acquisition.

(D) The program caught up with other programs within a month.

2. Why do the characters have abnormal appearance in this program?

(A) Because they look like funny.

(B) Because the target is under five years old.

(C) Because they mirror the real bodies of infants.

(D) Because phone calls poured in from audience.

3. Which of the following is NOT the reason the program has become so popular?

(A) It was developed based on the thorough studies of young kids.

(B) Kids under five cannot perceive the cultural differences between nations.

(C) Marketing plan of BBC was excellent.

(D) The show is broadcast in 27 countries.

Questions *4 ~ 6* are based on the following letter.

August 15, 2008
Mr. Les Gardner
level 30, One Pacific Place
55 Queensway, Hong Kong

Dear Mr. Gardner

I am pleased that you will be able to attend our Annual Sales Conference from October 20-23, 2008. All our representatives world- wide are planning to attend, most of whom you have already met.

Greg Larkin, with whom you spoke last December 16, is in charge of all conference logistics. He has prepared an attachment to this fax on which he has provided information about the weather in New York in October and recommendations for clothing. He will soon be sending you some information about activities in which you may wish to participate if you plan to be in New York the weekend before the conference.

We have reserved a block of rooms at the Sixth Avenue Hotel, about which we have had good reports from other visitors. Please fax the attached accomodations request form directly to the hotel by September 15, 2008.

Please book your own flights. Once you know the details, please fax the information to Greg so he can arrange to have you met at the airport. If you have any questions about travel or accomodations, please call Greg directly.

I am looking forward to seeing you in October.

Sincerely yours,

Tom Masterson

Manager

encl.

4. When will the conference be held?

(A) September 15, 2008

(B) August 15, 2008

(C) October 20-23, 2008

(D) December 16, 2008

5. Who is the coordinator of this conference?

(A) Mr. Les Gardner

(B) Mr. Greg Larkin

(C) Mr. Tom Masterson

(D) Not known

6. Which of the following is NOT correct?

(A) Mr. Gardner has ever met other representatives world-wide.

(B) Attendant in this conference can have a personal weekend plan if he wants.

(C) Accommodation request form is to be sent by the day of conference opening.

(D) The reserved hotel proves to be good from other visitors.

Picture A Better World
International Photographic Competition
On the Environment 2009 - 2010

At Canon, we understand that to make this world a better place, we must focus on the things we hope to change, as well as the things we want to save. That's why we are proud to sponsor the third International Photographic Competition on the Environment. An opportunity for you to show us the world as you see it. The good and the bad. The beauty and the despair.

PRIZES TO BE AWARDED

1. Gold Prize(one entrant)   diploma, US$20,000
   Silver Prize(one entrant)   diploma, US$10,000
   Bronze Prize(three entrants)   diploma, US$5,000
   Honorary Mention(seventy entrants)   diploma
2. The Canon Special Prize
3. The International Photographic Council Scholarship
4. The Digital Camera Special Prize

Canon products will be presented as supplementary prizes to all the above prizewinners. Payment of subsequent taxation on prizes is not the organizers responsibility.

AWARDS CEREMONY AND EXHIBITION
The Prizewinner and Winners of Honorary Mention will be announced at an awards ceremony that will be held in September 2010. Winner of the Gold Prize will be invited to attend the awards presentation ceremony at the expense of the organizers. Winners of the Special Prizes will also be invited to awards ceremony.

7. What is the purport of this photographic competition?

(A) To change the manufacturing process.

(B) To safeguard nature for a better environment.

(C) To save the bad and the despair.

(D) To advertise Canon Products.

8. Which of the following is correct?

(A) Only Winners of Special Prize will be invited to awards ceremony.

(B) All prizewinners will be invited to attend the awards presentation ceremony at the expense of the organizers.

(C) Payment of taxation is in charge of the organizers.

(D) All prizewinners will receive Canon products as supplementary prizes.

The elderly man ahead of me on the supermarket checkout line had trouble keep-ing up with the cashier as she rapidly rang up the prices on the register. "Miss, why do you go so fast?" he asked. "I hardly know which items you've already done.", "Sir, think of me as a dentist," she replied brightly. "The faster I do it, the less it hurts."

By keeping clear of allergic environmental triggers, you can lessen the chance of setting off an asthma attack.

- Avoid cigarette smoke.
- Reduce humidity by airing bedrooms daily.
- Vacuum carpets daily. Always dust with a damp cloth or use the vacuum cleaner attachment.
- Wash bedding every week at 60 degrees and vacuum the mattress every time you change the sheets.
- Buy washable children's soft toys, or failing that, place them in a plastic bag in the freezer overnight.
- Keep cats and dogs out of children's bedrooms.

9. What is the best title of this passage?
   (A) Cutting the asthma risk
   (B) Non-smoking
   (C) Protecting animal
   (D) Use of vacuum cleaner

10. Why should we keep cats and dogs out of children's bedrooms?
   (A) Because they are dangerous for children.
   (B) Because they get the bedroom dirty.
   (C) Because they trigger asthma.
   (D) Because they bite the mattress.

One day a small boy tried to lift a heavy stone, but couldn't budge it. His father, watching, finally said, "Are you sure you're using all your strength?" "Yes, I am!" the boy cried.
"No, you're not," said the father. "You haven't asked me to help you."

A USED CAR OF MY SON

We live less than 400 meters from secondary school, but my son proudly drove there in a car he bought with his own money. A typical first car, it had lots of problems and was sometimes slow to start.

One morning I was surprised to see it still in front of the house, so after school I asked him about it. "I had to get to school early," he said, "so I just ran."

11. Why did he run to school without his car that day?
   (A) His car needed repairing.
   (B) He thought that running would be faster than driving.
   (C) His school is close to his house within 400 meters.
   (D) He keeps his car proudly in his house.

12. Which one best describes his car?
   (A) Father bought it for his son as a birthday gift.
   (B) It is a typical first car with little problem.
   (C) It is slow to start on a cold weather.
   (D) It seems to be a used car with a cheap price.

To offset the depression I felt at reaching my 40th birthday, I treated myself to a new hairdo and a new outfit. Walking down the street, I was flattered when two young men waved at me, saying something in Spanish. Acting the proper lady, I ignored them, tossing my head haughtily as I marched resolutely onward. A third man tried to speak to me as I strode past his car. He finally leaned his head out the window and yelled, "Ma'am, they're trying to tell you-you're walking in their wet cement."

Looking for the perfect pet, one that never slobbers or barks in the night? Meet Sony's TERA, a 30-cm-tall plastic pup, powered by computer chip, that can walk, sit, lie down, even raise a paw in the air. Stroke a sensor on its head, and TERA wags its tail; throw a ball, and a digital camera in its snout will track it. A remote control turns it left or right. Available at www.world.sony.com/robot/ for $2,500, TERA costs more than most purebreds. But it doesn't shed, can't dig holes in the yard and needs no food or water. Best of all, you never have to clean up after it.

13. In what feature is TERA the same as the real dog?
   (A) TERA never slobbers or barks in the night.
   (B) TERA digs holes in the yard.
   (C) TERA is fed with some food.
   (D) TERA wags its tail when we touch a sensor on the head.

14. Which one is implied in the price of $2,500?
   (A) Cheaper than the dog with good blood.
   (B) TERA is expensive but worth keeping it.
   (C) We need to pay such amount of money to feed and clean the TERA.
   (D) A dog of purebred is better than the TERA.

When noted American economist Milton Friedman visited Hong Kong, a reporter asked him, "If an economist assumes the presidency of the United States, you for instance, would it be possible to set the country's economy in order?"

With a smile and without a moment's hesitation, Friedman replied, "No. For I would then be a politician."

Questions *15 – 16* are based on the following statistical research

Helping Hands

A volunteer works without pay. Volunteers try to help the sick or the homeless. Volunteers work for the Red Cross and the Cancer Society. Volunteers help to raise money for good causes. Volunteers work for politicians and fire departments. The table shows the age groups of volunteers.

age group	volunteers rate
14-17	58%
18-24	43%
25-44	63%
45-64	54%
65+	41%

15. Which of the following needs fewer volunteers than others?

(A) The Red Cross and the Cancer Society

(B) Raising money for good causes

(C) Political campaign

(D) Shopping mall

16. Which age group has the highest rate of volunteers?

(A) 14–17

(B) 18–24

(C) 25–44

(D) 45–64

Top 5 Family Vacations

When it's time for a family getaway this summer, will you pack goggles and fins, a city map and comfy shoes, or cough drops to soothe your sore throat after a screamer of a roller coaster ride? Here are the places 1,200 adults say they'll head to most with their kids in 2010. (They were allowed to give more than one answer):

Historic sites : 29%

Theme parks : 35%

Oceans and beaches : 31%

Fishing and other outdoor activities : 30%

Family reunions : 27%

17. Which answer has the second highest percentage?

(A) Oceans and beaches

(B) Historic sites

(C) Family reunions

(D) Theme parks

18. Which of the following is correct?

(A) 1,200 adults have answered the questions.

(B) Most people have a vacation plan to go without their kids.

(C) A respondent should give only one answer in this survey.

(D) People do not like to meet their family.

WELCOME TO
ADVENTURE AMERICA R.V. INC.

Recreational

Vehicle Rental & Manufacturing

Come see the very best the U.S.A. has to offer.

Discover the Western United States landscape with the luxuries of a R.V. Adventure America, and is centrally located in the heart of California's gold country. We have several motor home rental plans to choose from Class A, Class C, Travel trailers, and Van conversions. Our units sleep 4 to 8 people with all the comforts of your own home. All motor homes include thermostat controlling heat and air conditioning, plush interiors, complete bathrooms and fully equipped kitchens with microwave ovens, Televisions and generators. Please contact Adventure America for your Recreational needs.

ADVENTURE AMERICA R.V. INC.

2361 Manning Street, Sacramento, CA 95815

(916) 567-1009 * FAX (916) 567-1013

19. In which part in the U.S. is the company located?
    (A) Eastern part
    (B) Western part
    (C) Northern part
    (D) Southern part

20. Who would make the best use of the service from the Adventure America?
    (A) A family having a recreational trip and staying in a luxurious hotel.
    (B) A person expecting to have a business trip.
    (C) A family of 7 members planning a recreational trip.
    (D) A couple planning to have a recreational trip.

21. Which is NOT provided in the vehicles?
    (A) Telephone box
    (B) Thermostat controlled heat
    (C) Bathrooms
    (D) Kitchen

A missionary found himself face-to-face with raging lion in a jungle. "I'm going to eat you," roared the lion "Prepare for death." At that, the missionary dropped to his knees and prayed more fervently than he ever had before. Then, cautiously peeking through his fingers, he saw the lion also kneeling, with front paws covering his eyes. Looking toward heaven, the missionary exclaimed, "Isn't it wonderful... to think paws and snarled. Hold your tongue! I'm saying grace."

Questions *22 – 23* refer to the following advertisement.

A TEENY PRICE ON OUR
SMALLEST NOTEBOOK COMPUTER

Crown's 320SLi weighs only 3.6 pounds and is only 1.25" thick - about half of the size of comparable notebooks. Yet it's fully functional and powerful enough to handle any mainstream business application anywhere. No wonder notebook users - and notebook experts - love this marvel of Crown engineering. Now it's easier than ever to pick one up and start your own love affair.

---

22. Which feature is NOT advertised?

    (A) light weight

    (B) cheap price

    (C) thin

    (D) useful for student

23. Who would probably buy this product?

    (A) applicants

    (B) businessmen

    (C) lovers

    (D) teachers

A man went to his pastor and confided that he found life empty.

"Why?" asked the pastor.

"Because the woman I love has just rejected my proposal of marriage."

"Don't let that get you down." said the pastor brightly. "A woman's 'no' often means 'yes."

"But she didn't say, 'No,' replied the man sadly. She said, phooey.'"

Negotiating

FIRST BOOKS FOR BUSINESS

Created for people with no time to waste, negotiating is your inside guide to the art of give-and-take. You'll learn all about the importance of body language, argument style, staying focused, and much more. And soon you'll be getting exactly the deals you want.

24. What is NOT learned from this book?

(A) the gesture while you are talking

(B) paying attention to the focus

(C) suggesting a best price

(D) argument style

25. For whom was this book written?

(A) an expert in negotiating at a business deal

(B) a busy student who studies in a body language course

(C) a secretary who helps a marketing manager

(D) a business man who wants a successful negotiation

> I discovered at an early age that most of the differences between average people and great people can be explained in three words- and then some. They were considerate and thoughtful of others, and then some. They met their obligations and responsibilities fairly and squarely, and then some. They were good friends to their friends, and then some. They could be counted on in an emergency, and then some.

The Music Maker with 12 Songs

Made in Belarus $45.99 (plus shipping/handling and sales tax where applicable)

Anyone, regardless of skill, can learn to play beautiful music with the Music Maker, made in Belarus. Just slide a songsheet under the strings and pluck the string above each note - it's that easy! The Music Maker represents an excellent opportunity to introduce children to the joys of music and it lets them immediately play beautiful music.

This gives them the confidence to want to learn more about music.

Songs included:

Twinkle, Twinkle, Little Star

Rock A Bye Baby

Minuet (Bach)

My Country Tis Of Thee

Brahm's Lullaby

Baa, Baa, Black Sheep

Daisy

Clementine

Yankee Doodle

Row, Row, Row Your Boat

Jesu, Joy Of Man's Desiring

Eensie, Weensie Spider

26. Which of the following best describes the instrument?

(A) an automatic easy–to–use song player

(B) an instrument useful for composing

(C) an easy instrument that anyone can play

(D) a kind of professional instrument

27. What type of the instruments does the Music Maker look like?

(A) a percussion instrument

(B) a string instrument

(C) a keyboard instrument

(D) a wind instrument

28. How can you play the Music Maker?

(A) Just slide the song–sheet under the string and push the button

(B) Just key in the note in the song–sheet and pluck the string

(C) Just insert the song–sheet under the string and use the finger on the string

(D) Just slide the song–sheet under the Music Maker and adjust the volume.

Answering an ad for employment, a young student arrived early for an interview, but found several applicants ahead of him. He wrote a quick note and handed it to the receptionist, telling her it was important that her boss receive the note at once. She smiled as she read it, then took it to the boss. "Dear Sir," the note read. "I am tenth in line. Please don't make any decision until you've interviewed me."

He got the jod.

November 14, 1998

Mr. Thomas Rollins
666 East 17th Street
Santa Ana, California 92701

Dear Tom,

Thank you for taking time out of your day to discuss some ideas regarding my job search. Your input and information has been of tremendous help. I have been gratified and deeply touched by all of the help and support that I have received. The information and support which you gave me are truly appreciated.

I have tried to call both John and Sherry Bradbury, but have not yet spoken to them. I am sure I will talk to them in the near future. I have had a couple of meetings since our luncheon, and I incorporated some of your suggestions into my discussions with the persons I met with. Your comments were very helpful, and seemed to make a favorable impression.

Again, thank you very much. If ever there is anything I can do for you, please let me know.

Very truly yours,

Richard E. Hart

29. Why has this letter been written?
   (A) to order an item
   (B) to consult an expert for a job search
   (C) to express the appreciation for the help
   (D) to ask a favor meet John and Sherry Bradbury

30. What is a correct situation on Richard's job search?

(A) He had a telephone conversation with Sherry Bradbury.

(B) Tom's advice was very helpful.

(C) He successfully found a job with the help of Tom.

(D) He decided to be any help for Tom rather than find a job.

31. What did the writer do after meeting Tom?

(A) He had a couple of meetings with John.

(B) He made good use of Tom's suggestions at some meetings.

(C) He made some mistake at the meeting.

(D) He was deeply touched by the meetings after luncheon.

Questions 32~35 refer to the following article.

INSTALLING DETECTING SYSTEM AT THE BORDER

With some 60% of illegal drugs entering America from the south, federal authorities are installing high-tech military gear on the U.S.-Mexican border. The equipment, starting with special X-ray scanners, will also include gamma-ray and positron-emission screening systems, all developed in the cold war to detect Soviet nuclear warheads. General Barry McCaffrey, the U.S. drug-policy chief, said the plan should cut the traffic's volume by forcing smugglers to use sea routes. The U.S. also indicted Ramon Arellano Felix, one of the Tijuana drug cartel's most violent leaders, and will place him on the FBI's 10 Most Wanted List.

---

32. Where is the equipment installed?

(A) U.S.–Mexican border

(B) New York Harbor

(C) Alaska airport

(D) U.S.–Canada border

33. What was the original use of the scanning equipment?

    (A) chest checker at health care center

    (B) detecting nuclear warheads

    (C) detecting the imitated money

    (D) detecting the illegal drugs

34. After installing the gear, which route would the smugglers use?

    (A) express mail

    (B) airborne

    (C) land

    (D) sea

35. What did the U.S. government try to reduce the illegal drugs?

    (A) The U.S. provided the neighboring nations with the scanning equipment.

    (B) The U.S. improved the detecting ability on the south border.

    (C) The U.S. increased the number of detecting dogs.

    (D) The U.S. advised the cartel leader Felix to finish his business

> Once, at a story conference, Charlie, an unpredictable eccentric, kept slapping at a fly buzzing around his head. Calling for a swatter, he swung several times but missed. At last, the offender settled down before him, and Chaplin lifted the swatter for the death blow. He paused, looked carefully at the fly and lowered the swatter. "Why didn't you swat him?" he was asked. Shrugging typically, Chaplin said, "It wasn't the same fly."

Questions *36 - 37* refer to the following passage.

> ## Tommy William's holidays special
>
> The Hilton hotel has prepared a truly special event for you to celebrate these holidays with your family to the tune of Tommy William's playing and songs. He is a world renowned pianist. On Sunday, December 27 and Monday, December 28 from 11:30 am at Swan Hall, delight with a mouth-watering seasonal menu, participate with your kids in games.

36. What instrument does Tommy Williams play?

    (A) Saxophone

    (B) Flute

    (C) Piano

    (D) Clarinet

37. How many nights will Tommy William perform?

    (A) One

    (B) Two

    (C) Four

    (D) Seven

A minister passed along to a beginning preacher a trick he used when he saw the congregation nodding a bit, "I suddenly say them, last night I held another man 's wife in my arms. When everyone sits up, shocked, I continue, It was my own dear mother."

The young preacher thought he'd try it. The next Sunday when most members of his congregation were drowsing, he said in a loud voice, "You know, last night I held another man's wife in my arms." Stunned the congregation sat bolt upright and stared, whereupon the preacher stammered, "Oh, dear-I've forgotten who she was."

Questions 38 - 39 refer to the following passage.

Emergencies

Dial 211 for the police and 911 for the fire and ambulance. The hotel front desk or hotel manager can arrange for a doctor or ambulance. In the event of a medical emergency on the street, ask a policeman or passing pedestrian for assistance. Police boxes can be found on every major street. Tourists would be well advised to keep the phone number of their consulate or embassy with them. The Lost and Found Center is run by New York Metropolitan Police Bureau.

---

38. For whom is the information intended?

(A) hotel guest

(B) assistant

(C) policeman

(D) operator

39. Where can you find the police box?

(A) in the hotel

(B) at the consulate

(C) on every major street

(D) near the hotel

When I discovered to my dismay, that my aged great-aunt still climbed over the garden fence to visit her next-door neighbor, I asked her why she didn't take the less dangerous route down the driveway and the street.

"Look," came her sharp reply, "I'll be ninety at the end of this year and I'm running out of time."

Questions *40-42* refer to the following press release.

Paradise, Inc. has announced plans to purchase Contemporary Style Corporation, publisher of Eastern Life and other magazines, for $285 million. Eastern Life, a regional magazine that has a monthly circulation of 3.4 million, was attractive to Paradise because of its high percentage of female readers, said Erick Burtman, a Paradise spokesman. "Paradise does not have a women's magazine and this one has a 81 percent female readership, so we're expanding into a new area," he said.

40. What percentage of the male readership of Eastern Life is?
(A) 50 percent
(B) 19 percent
(C) 13 percent
(D) 81 percent

41. Who is the present owner of Eastern Life?
(A) Erick Burtman
(B) Paradise, Inc.
(C) the 81 percent male readership
(D) Contemporary Style Corporation

42. What's the new area Paradise moving into?
(A) magazine publishing
(B) the women's market
(C) the men's the market
(D) television

Questions 43 – 45 refer to the following table.

Survey of Factory Personnel

Age	Men	Women
Under 25	10	26
26 - 35	34	44
36 - 50	38	10
Over 51	13	0
Marital Status		
Married	54	20
Divorced, Widowed, Separated	10	32
Single	31	28

43. The majority are

(A) married women over 36.

(B) married men.

(C) divorced, widowed, or separated women, ages 36 – 50.

(D) married men, age 26–35.

44. More women than men are

(A) between 36 and 50 years old.

(B) married.

(C) single.

(D) divorced, widowed, or separated.

45. There are fewer men than women

(A) under 35 years of age.

(B) over 50 years of age.

(C) who are married.

(D) aged 36–50.

Questions *46 – 48* refer to the following report.

An annual combination of negative external factors presented us with challenges of a rare severity. We not only managed to meet these challenges, but were able to record improved statistics. In the past years, our proudest achievement was that we were able to place into action programs which should provide the basis for a solid earnings expansion in the years ahead.

46. The mood of this report is
   (A) initially negative, but it ends on a positive note.
   (B) completely positive.
   (C) mostly negative, but with some positive ideas.
   (D) positive for the future.

47. The company was at a disadvantage because
   (A) of past performance.
   (B) of problems outside the company.
   (C) the basis had not previously been balanced.
   (D) of future expansion.

48. An example of a 'negative external factor' may be
   (A) personnel turnover.
   (B) a strike.
   (C) inflation.
   (D) management recognition.

In a crowded department store, a young couple was Christmas-shopping. In the hustle and bustle, the wife was separated from her husband. She turned to a guide, "I have lost my husband. Where can I ...?" Before she finished, the couldn't-care-less guide replied, "sorry to hear it, Madame. The funeral department is on the top floor."

Studio Center

Studio Center Closes at 6:00 p.m.

TRAM RIDE

Get a behind the scenes look at the world's largest working movie studio. With 420 acres, you'll see hundreds of sets from your favorite motion pictures and television shows. Experience an 8.3 Earthquake, Jaws, King Kong and much more! Last Tram Departs at 4:15 p.m.

JURASSIC PARK

Come face to face with Triceratops, Brachiosaurus, and Velociraptro in an interactive exhibit. Open from 9 a.m. to 6 p.m.

THE E.T. ADVENTURE

Quick! Hop about your bicycle and fly with E.T. on an adventure of a dream. Open from 9:00 a.m. to 6:00 p.m.

BACKDRAFT

Feel the fury of a raging firestorm as Ron Howard's blockbuster movie roars to life. A true five-alarm thriller, BACKDRAFT: 10,000 Degrees of Live Excitement. Open from 9:00 a.m. to 6:00 p.m. Last show begin at 5:45 p.m.

49. When does the Studio Center close?

(A) at 5:00 p.m.

(B) at 6:00 p.m.

(C) at 7:00 p.m.

(D) at 9:00 p.m.

50. When does the last show begin in BACKDRAFT?

    (A) at 4:15 p.m.

    (B) at 6:00 p.m.

    (C) at 5:30 p.m.

    (D) at 5:45 p.m.

51. Which one can't you experience at this studio center?

    (A) monstrous animal

    (B) dinosaur

    (C) famous comedian

    (D) bike tour

52. Which of the following is NOT described?

    (A) Feel the fantastic ecstasy of the three—dimensional world.

    (B) Experience an 8.3 Earthquake, Jaws, King Kong during the TRAM RIDE.

    (C) The last show of TRAM riding begins at 4:15 p.m.

    (D) BACKDRAFT is a true five—alarm thriller.

It was the last day of our vacation, and my husband informed me that he was going to get in a final game of golf. I had the tedious task of packing and organizing for the return trip. To make matters worse, he asked me to delay doing the laundry until after his game so that I could wash and pack his dirty golf clothes.

As the day wore on, I became more and more impatient. I couldn't pack until I did the wash, and I couldn't wash until he returned. I visualized an evening of drudgery instead of enjoying the final hours with family and friends.

By the time he walked through the door, relatives had already gathered to say good-by. They were shocked speechless when my first words to my husband were, "Get your clothes off! I've been waiting all day."

Part-Time Work As Secretary

ARE YOU UNDERSTAFFED?
Do you have full-time secretarial needs,
but only a part-time budget?

Wouldn't it be great to have a part-time secretary with all the skills and experience of a full-time secretary? Here are some of my skills and abilities:

Get things done and handle a variety of tasks EFFICIENTLY.

Organize my time and complete tasks quickly and ACCURATELY.

Work very well independently--am an ambitious SELF-STARTER.

Am super CONSCIENTIOUS.

Am a skilled typist--90 WORDS PER MINUTE.

Am thorough in RECORD KEEPING.

Show painstaking attention to DETAIL.

Am attractive and WELL-GROOMED.

I have a STRONG and very COMPETENT secretarial background, as well as experience in SUPERVISION. I have worked as a secretary/administrative assistant in a variety of areas.

BONUS: I love to be BUSY.

I AM LOOKING FOR PART-TIME SECRETARIAL WORK AND WILL PROVIDE YOU WITH TOP-NOTCH QUALITY SERVICE. IF YOU ARE LOOKING FOR THE BEST, WHY NOT GIVE ME A CALL?

Bobbi Gutentag

100 Reed Street, Lakewood, Colorado 80215

You can reach me weekdays between 8:00-10:00 a.m. at 231-4765

53. What is the purpose of this letter?

    (A) To ask for a full—time job

    (B) To ask for help from secretary

    (C) To seek a person as a secretary

    (D) To seek a part—time job

54. According to the letter, which is NOT the feature of the writter?

    (A) He is well—experienced and likes to be busy.

    (B) He has worked as a secretary assistant in various areas.

    (C) He is well—dressed and very faithful to his work.

    (D) He cannot be satisfied with part—time salary and wants some bonus.

55. How can the writter be characterized?

    (A) He looks ambitious and positive.

    (B) He looks sophisticated.

    (C) He looks childish and simple.

    (D) He looks reflective and introspective.

Questions 56 ~ 58 are based on the following advertisement.

World Offers flying from New York

If you're planning a trip to London, take advantage of our 'London in the Summer' hotel promotion and experience four-star style on a two-star budget. For complete details of these unbelievably low fares, destinations, terms and conditions see your travel agent, or call British Airways at 1-800-368-7373.

These fares valid for travel commencing between June 16th, and August 31st, 1999.

1-800-368-7373

These are the British Airways World Offers available from New York.

These are one-way fares based on a round-trip purchase.

London	$299	Genoa	$430
Amsterdam	$359	Helsinki	$425
Athens	$435	Istanbul	$440
Barcelona	$405	Lisbon	$390
Basel	$390	Lyon	$405
Bologna	$430	Madrid	$405
Copenhagen	$405	Malta	$591
Dublin	$309	Marseille	$405
Geneva	$390	Milan	$430

56. Which of the date is NOT valid for the special service?

(A) July 1st

(B) June 5th

(C) July 27th

(D) August 2nd

57. If you want to get a round trip ticket for Athens, how much does it cost?

(A) $435

(B) $218

(C) $870

(D) $359

58. Which of the following is correct?

(A) There is a special star exhibition in the hotel.

(B) Although you start from any place, you can take advantage of this service.

(C) For complete details of these services, you can call British Airways.

(D) The round-trip fare for Geneva is $390.

PEOPLE AND PLACES

Photo Contest - $4,000 in Prize!

Are your photographs good enough to be in a magazine? Here's an opportunity to find out. Enter the PEOPLE AND PLACES Amateur Photography Contest. We will give away $4,000 in prize money - $2,000 for first prize, $1,000 for second, $500 for third, $300 for fourth, and $200 for fifth. In addition, we'll put the photo that wins first prize on the cover of our May 1st issue.

The judges are Tracy Black of PEOPLE AND PLACES, Catherine Steriade, the owner of Steriade Photo Shops, and professional photographer Billy Burke. They will choose the best photos, and we will send letters to all the winners on April 1st.

◦ Contest Rules ◦

1. This contest is for amateurs only.
2. Send only one photo. It can be any size.
   Put your name and address on the back.
3. Photos can be either black-and-white or color on any subject.
4. The deadline is February 15th.
5. PEOPLE AND PLACES will not return the photos.
6. Send your entry to Photo Contest,
   PEOPLE AND PLACES
   600 South Avenue, Midvale.

---

59. Who can enter the contest?

(A) Judge

(B) Amateur

(C) Professor

(D) Tracy Black

60. When will you know the final result?

(A) On May 1st

(B) On April 1st

(C) On February 15th

(D) On March 10th

61. How many prizes will there be?

(A) Five prizes

(B) Three prizes

(C) Four prizes

(D) One prize

62. Which of the following is NOT correct?

(A) Send only one photo in any size.

(B) Only black—and—white photo can be allowed.

(C) Due day is February 15th.

(D) The photo will not be returned to the applicant.

A statistician who had never taken care of his four small, energetic children by himself reluctantly promised to look after them one Saturday afternoon while his wife went shopping. When she returned, he gave her a note that read: "Dried tears- 11 times. Tied shoelaces- 15 times. Blew up toy balloons- 5 per child. Average life of each balloon- 10 seconds. Warned children not to run across street- 26 times. Children insisted on running across street- 26 times. Number of Saturdays I will go through this again- 0."

Questions 63 - 64 are based on the following table.

Schedules
Voyager Airlines - Arrivals and Departures

Arrivals

From	Flight No.	Due	Status	Gate No.
Tokyo	310	10:30	10:50	12
Vancouver	643	10:45	ON TIME	20
Moscow	19	10;45	11:15	8
Santiago	10	11:00	ON TIME	6
Miami	83	11:10	ON TIME	11
Bogota	591	11:15	11:30	14
Cairo	175	11:20	11:45	10

Departures

To	Flight No.	Leaves	Statue	Gate No.
Quebec	211	10:30	ON TIME	9
New York	3	10:45	ON TIME	7
London	6	11:00	ON TIME	13
Mexico City	778	11:00	11:20	21
Paris	687	11:15	ON TIME	15
Calgary	115	11:20	11:45	10
Manila	26	11:30	12:00	9

63. When was Flight 778 scheduled to leave?

    (A) 11:00   (B) 10:30

    (C) 11:20   (D) 10:45

64. What's the final destination of Flight 115?

    (A) Tokyo   (B) Miami

    (C) Calgary   (D) Quebec

Questions *65~67* refer to the following report.

Report to Shoppers

by Betty Freeman

Do you want to save money on fruit and vegetables? These days, who doesn't? Then I can recommend the new Food's Market, next to the 5th Street railroad station. It's only open from 9 to 12 Monday, Tuesday, and Friday mornings, but you should take the trouble to go there.

There's a lot of fruit, and the prices are very good. Yesterday I bought five melons for only 89cents each. The same melons were $1.45 each in Farmer's Supermarket.

At this time of year they only have a few fresh vegetables, but I found some beautiful lettuce for 59cents, and peas were only 99cents a pound. Not many supermarkets in this area have prices that low, even during their weekend specials.

There are some things that I don't like. They don't have many dairy products. Last week they didn't have any butter... Also, you should shop early. The good things sell out fast.

---

65. How much money did Betty pay for five melons yesterday?

(A) 89 cents

(B) 99 cents

(C) 1 dollar and 45 cents

(D) 4 dollars and 45 cents

66. Why should you shop early?

(A) Because the good things sell out early.

(B) Because the fresh vegetables are withered.

(C) Because they don't have many dairy products.

(D) Because the railroad station is crowded afternoon.

67. What doesn't Betty like about the market?

(A) They don't have fresh vegetables.

(B) They close the shop too early.

(C) They don't sell a lot of milk and cheese.

(D) You should take the trouble to go there.

Questions *68 ~ 69* are based on the following story.

A Parking Problem

My husband and I had decided to buy a new house, and I'd made an appointment to see our bank manager. I'd never met him before and I was a bit nervous. I drove into town and I was lucky enough to find a parking space outside the bank. I'd just started reversing into the space when another car drove into it. I was furious! I opened my window and shouted at the other driver. He ignored me and walked away. It took me twenty minutes to find another space. As soon as I had parked the car, I rushed back to the bank. I was ten minutes late for my interview. I went to the manager's office, knocked and walked in. The manager was sitting behind his desk. He was the man who had taken my parking space!

---

68. Why was she late for the appointment?

(A) Because she could not find a parking lot.

(B) Because she had an interview.

(C) Because she bought a new house.

(D) Because she shouted at the other driver.

69. When she saw the manager, how would she feel?

(A) She was satisfied.

(B) She was shy and blushed.

(C) She was frightened.

(D) She was exhausted.

The position of women in American society is sometimes misunderstood by those from other countries. An example may illustrate. The wife of an American professor in Europe, deprived of her electric washer and dryer with which many American homes are equipped, bundled up her washing every week to send to the local laundry. The bundle was rather large, and the family had no car. Therefore it was logical, from the American point of view, for the husband to put the bundle on his bicycle and pedal off to the laundry with it every Monday morning before going to his classes at the university. The professor's wife soon discovered that the neighbors' tongues were busy. One woman whom she knew better than the rest finally approached her. "You shouldn't do that, you know," she said. "It gives people the wrong idea."

"I don't understand," said the professor's wife. "I think it is very kind of my husband to take the laundry for me. It is a heavy bundle, and I have a lot of housework to do. In America it is not beneath the dignity of a professor to help his wife."

"Oh, it is not your husband that people are taking about," said the neighbor. "They are talking about you. Your husband works hard all day and people say you are not considerate of him. When he is going to a hard day of work he shouldn't have to carry the washing first. That's your job."

70. Where did this happening occur?
   (A) It occurred in America.
   (B) It occurred in Europe.
   (C) It occurred at the university.
   (D) It occurred at a laundry.

71. Why were the neighbors' tongues busy?
   (A) Because they thought wife should be responsible for the housework.
   (B) Because Professor should not carry some laundry for his dignity.
   (C) Because the electric washer was out of order for a long time.
   (D) Because they had a lot of houseworks.

Questions *72 – 74* are based on the following diagram.

Education in Asia

United Nations Data on School Life Expectancy
(years spent in formal education).
Note: Many Asian nations were not included in this report.

School Life Expectancy (SLE)

(years of formal education)

Nation/Region	Total	Male	Female
Hong Kong	12.6	12.6	12.7
Indonesia	10	10.4	9.5
Japan	14	14.2	13.8
Korea, Republic of	14.5	15.1	13.9
Laos	6.9	8.2	5.7
Mongolia	7.2	6.2	8.1

◈ **School Life Expectancy in Select Asian Nations/Regions** ◈

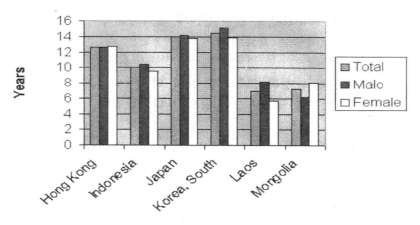

72. In which nation is female's SLE longer than that of male?

(A) Korea

(B) Japan

(C) Laos

(D) Mongolia

73. In this diagram, what does 'Total' mean?

(A) Mean

(B) Sum

(C) Multiple

(D) Difference

74. Which one is NOT true about education in Asia?

(A) In Indonesia, female's SLE is 9.5 years.

(B) Korea has the longest formal education term.

(C) All of Asian nations were selected in this report.

(D) It is in Laos that child has the shortest SLE.

A successful, unmarried career woman had a married sister named Joan, whose life centered on her husband and children. One day, the mother of the two women was talking to the single daughter. "You're not married." she said. "You don't have a man to take care of you. What's going to become of you?"

"Mother, for heaven's sake." the unmarried woman snapped. "I'm living exactly as I like. I make plenty of money, and I can spend it on myself. I don't have to worry about what some man wants. I go to Europe twice a year. I entertain. I have all the friends I want, and I'm not tied down to housework or kids. My life is glamorous and wonderful."

There was a pause and then the mother said, "I know. Don't tell Joan"

Questions 75 - 76 are based on the following advertisement.

Inside and out, a Jaguar is a thing of beauty. Prized for its eye-caching design, today's Jaguar evokes equally high praise for its outstanding quality and performance. No wonder Jaguar owners pamper their vehicles. And no wonder so many savvy people yearn for a Jaguar to call their own. Now, with the new Jaguar Select Edition 6-year/100,000-mile warranty, a pre-owned Jaguar is an exceptional value. Consider joining the Jaguar family today and inheriting a masterpiece.

JAGUAR
SELECT EDITION
PreOwned Automobiles

1-800-4-JAGUAR

---

75. What is this advertisement about?

(A) It's about wild animal.

(B) It's about masterpiece.

(C) It's about automobile.

(D) It's about eye-protector.

76. What is the exceptional value of the new Jaguar Select Edition?

(A) It is prominent quality and performance.

(B) It has noticeable design.

(C) It has 6-year/100,000-mile warranty.

(D) It is beautiful inside as well as outside.

100 PAGES
OF FREE ADVICE
FOR ANYONE WISHING
TO VISIT ALASKA

What's Alaska really like? Where should I stay? How should I dress? Or get around? There's a lot of mystery surrounding Alaska. And every year, people interested in visiting here start asking questions like these.

Fortunately, we've just put together the definitive answer. It's called the Alaska and Canada's Yukon Vacation Planner. This beautiful 100-page book is the official guide to Alaska, prepared by the State of Alaska. And it's free when you simply fill out the attached card or write to the address below.

The Vacation Planner is filled with facts, figures, maps, tour information, color photographs, and personal reflections. In short, it offers a wealth of practical advice you'll put to use.

We want you to discover the timeless beauty and ancient spirit in Alaska. So please take our advice. Send for your free Vacation Planner now. It could lead to the most important travel decision you'll ever make.

Write to: Alaska Division of Tourism,
　　　　　Pouch E-401,
　　　　　Juneau, Alaska 99811.
Or call toll free (800) 228-0087.

77. What is the title of this book?

(A) Alaska and Canada's Yukon Vacation Planner

(B) Tour Information

(C) State of Alaska

(D) Mystery Surrounding Alaska

78. How can you get the book?

(A) We can get it by buying it in a bookstore.

(B) We can get it by sending the attached card.

(C) We can get it by traveling through Alaska.

(D) We can get it by answering the questions.

79. Which of the following is correct?

(A) If you want a free travel, only fill out the card.

(B) If you call, telephone charges should be paid.

(C) This is a theoretical textbook about Alaska.

(D) The book is published by the State of Alaska.

Three absent-minded professors were sitting in a railroad station waiting for a train. They were so absorbed in thought that they failed to notice the arrival of the train. Suddenly one of them noticed it as it started to pull out, and they all rushed for it. Two of them caught the train. A bystander consoled the third who missed it.

"You shouldn't fell bad," he said, "At least two of you made it."

"Yes, I know," replied the professor, "but those two came to see me off."

··· from

NATIONAL GEOGRAPHIC,

your source

for unforgettable

journeys

When you join the National Geographic Society, you'll journey to secret corners and cosmopolitan cities... to vast plains teeming with wildlife... to the mysterious ocean depths. You'll enjoy people and places you've visited before... or encountered for the first time. All captured in the brilliant photography that has made **NATIONAL GEOGRAPHIC** world-famous for more than a hundred years.

Start your journey of discovery now, and enjoy more pictures just as memorable. Simply complete and post the enclosed Membership Form with your fee today.

---

80. For whom is this advertisement needed?

(A) One who want to study geology

(B) One who want to make a journey of discovery

(C) One who want to enjoy excellent pictures

(D) One who want to explore the mysterious ocean depths

81. How can you get 'your source for unforgettable journeys'?

(A) You can get it for free.

(B) You can get it by calling on NATIONAL GEOGRAPHIC SOCIETY.

(C) You can get it by journey to secret corners.

(D) You can get it by posting the Membership Form with fee.

Questions 82 – 84 refer to the following calendar.

SUN	MON	TUE	WED	THE	FRI	SAT
1	2 CONTRACT TALKS –WESTBRAE CHEMICALS–	3 LUNCH WITH DON WARREN	4	5	6 9:00 AM STAFF MEETING	7
8	9	10 REVIEW EMERSON PROJECT	11	12	13 PREPARE DEMO FOR KEYSTONE	14
15	16 10:00 AM KEYSTONE DEMONSTRATION	17	18 DINNER W/SALLY	19	20	21
22	23 START BRACKEN PROJECT	24	25	26 9:30 AM MEETING WITH BILL AVERY	27	28
29	30 RUN MONTHLY REPORT					

82. What is scheduled for the second Tuesday of the month?

(A) A project review

(B) Lunch with Mr. Warren

(C) Preparation for a project demonstration

(D) Contract negotiations with Westbrae Chemicals

83. On which day of the week is a staff meeting scheduled?

(A) Monday

(B) Wednesday

(C) Thursday

(D) Friday

84. On which day is a new project scheduled to begin?

(A) Monday the 2nd

(B) Tuesday the 10th

(C) Sunday the 15th

(D) Monday the 23rd

Global Environment Deteriorating

A multinational environmental task force comprised of more than 500 environmental scientists and policymakers worldwide has published a report that concludes that the global environment is deteriorating at an alarming rate, despite pledges by the international community to give priority to conservation and pollution control efforts.

"It is entirely within the realm of human technology and ability to correct even the worst environmental problems. It is simply the will to act and the funds to implement these actions that are both vastly insufficient for the task..." says Abigail Rifkat, director of the International Program for Global Monitoring and lead author of the report.

Among the reports recommendations to the international community for halting the global environmental degradation are: developing alternative energy sources, distributing environmentally sound technologies worldwide, taking immediate action to protect fresh water sources, and improving environmental data collection.

---

85. What conclusion has been drawn by the report?

(A) The quality of the world's environment is worsening.

(B) The environmental policies of the developed world do not work in underdeveloped nations.

(C) Developing nations are contributing to global environmental problems at an increasing rate.

(D) Environmental problems in the industrialized world are worse than those in developing nations.

86. Which of the following is NOT a recommendation of the report?

(A) Improving environmental monitoring

(B) Developing new energy technologies

(C) Reducing the population growth rate

(D) Protecting sources of drinking water

87. What does Ms. Rifkat say about environmental problem?

(A) Governments should spend more money to study the environment.

(B) Human technology is not yet advanced enough to solve the most difficult environmental problems.

(C) Although humans can solve environmental problems, they are not making a strong enough effort to do so.

(D) Prevention of environmental problems is the most important task facing the human race today.

A Sri-Lankan professor went to London on his sabbatical leave. After three months he was tired of English food and went to a butcher shop to buy something to allay his homesickness.

"Have you brain?" he asked the butcher.

The butcher stared at him for a minute and then said, "If I had any, do you think I'd be working here?"

SPECIAL SAMPLE OFFER!

MODERN COOKING invites you to sample a FREE ISSUE without risk or obligation of any kind. Simply complete and return this card to receive your FREE ISSUE.

You will receive a bill for $16.97 for 11 more issues (for a total of 12). If you want to keep getting MODERN COOKING, pay the bill and you will SAVE 52% off the newsstand price AND get the new "Best of MODERN COOKING Recipe Collection"

-- absolutely FREE!

If you do not wish to subscribe, simply mark the bill "cancel," and that will be that.

The issue is yours to keep, FREE and forever.

PLEASE PRINT

Name : _____

Address : _____

City : _____ State : _____ Zip : _____

(Please allow 30 days for shipment of FREE issue).

88. How much is saved by subscribing for a full year?

(A) $ 11.00

(B) $ 16.97

(C) More than one fourth of the price

(D) More that one half of the price

89. What is included with a subscription?

(A) A kitchen knife

(B) A set of dishes

(C) A book of recipes

(D) A free cooking video

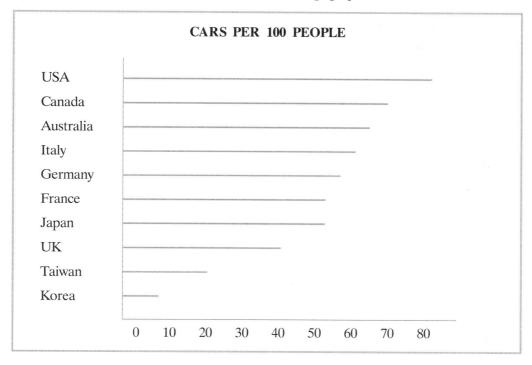

Questions *90 – 93* refer to the following graph.

CARS PER 100 PEOPLE

USA
Canada
Australia
Italy
Germany
France
Japan
UK
Taiwan
Korea

0 10 20 30 40 50 60 70 80

90. Which country has the greatest number of cars per 100 people?

(A) USA

(B) Italy

(C) UK

(D) Korea

91. What can be said about the number of cars per 100 people in Taiwan?

(A) It is more than twice that of Canada.

(B) It is less than half of that of Japan.

(C) It is double that of the United States.

(D) The rate is increasing faster than that of Korea.

92. Which countries have an equal number of cars per 100 people?

    (A) Taiwan and Korea

    (B) France and Japan

    (C) Italy and Germany

    (D) Canada and Australia

93. How many countries have more than 70 cars per 100 people?

    (A) 1

    (B) 2

    (C) 8

    (D) 10

Two hikers were walking through the woods when they suddenly confronted a giant bear. Immediately, one of the men took off his boots, pulled out a pair of track shoes and began putting them on. "What are you doing?" cried his companion. "We can't outrun that bear, even with jogging shoes."

"who cares about the bear?" the first hiker replied. All I have to worry about is outrunning you.

Questions 94 – 95 refer to the following advertisement.

A leading manufacturer of canned and frozen foodstuffs seeks

a

CHIEF OPERATING OFFICER

The candidate must:

* Hold a university degree, preferably in engineering or in a related field such as food science.

* Have a minimum of 10 years experience in managing production and related engineering functions.

* Be fluent in English and French. A command of Arabic is an asset.

Interested candidates meeting the above requirements are invited to send their resumes and/or call:

PO Box 57, Washington, DC 22186 Tel/Fax (202) 765-2818/2800

---

94. What must a successful candidate possess?

(A) Verbal and written fluency in German

(B) A class 'C' motor vehicle operator's license

(C) Ten years of production management experience

(D) A valid international engineering certificate

95. What is desirable, but not required, for the advertised position?

(A) Good public speaking skills

(B) Computer programing ability

(C) Facility with the Arabic language

(D) Knowledge of accounting principles

Questions *96 ~ 98* refer to the following passage.

Some Gulf States to Diversify

Gulf Arab oil producers Saudi Arabia, Kuwait, Bahrain, Oman, Qatar and the United Arab Emirates, members of the Gulf Cooperation Concil [GCC], plan to become major aluminum exporters and have spent more than $4 billion to expand existing aluminum smelters and develop new plants.

The region, now controlling nearly 6 percent of the world's total aluminum output, will control some 10 percent once the new projects are completed, according to a report published by the Gulf Organization for Industrial Consulting [GOIC]. Current exports exceed 520,000 tans annually, worth about $932 million, most of which is sold to Japan and South Korea.

The GOIC report concluded that "the future of the aluminum industry hinges on three basic factors: GCC cooperation in marketing and expansion, protection of the environment, and the establishment of and integrated aluminium industry that includes all types of products and the basic components to produce them."

---

96. According to the passage, what do some Gulf Arab states plan to do?

(A) Increase oil production

(B) Expand aluminum production

(C) Enlarge stockpiles of raw materials

(D) Control the world's supply of natural gas

97. What percentage of the world supply does the GOIC plan to provide?

(A) 6   (B) 10

(C) 90   (D) 94

98. On what does the GOIC say the future of the industry is dependent?

(A) Access to cheap aluminum supplies

(B) Continuation of current market trends

(C) Cooperation among the GCC member states

(D) Relaxation of current environmental restrictions

Don't Leave Home Without It

Unlike ordinary telephone cards that use magnetic stripes to hold information, 'smart cards' -wallet-sized plastic cards with embedded computer microprocessors-use a fingernail-sized microprocessor that can communicate with other computers. The microchips currently in use hold more than 80 times more information than magnetic stripes and can be divided into separate parts, which can perform several different functions.

Nearly a million chip-based cash replacement cards are in use from Spain to Denmark, charged with value by consumers at automatic teller machines. Versatility will improve as chip designers concentrate more computing power into smaller, cheaper microprocessors, and as companies adapt their cards for use on the global Internet. Doctors, hospitals, law enforcement officials, transit authorities and motor vehicle departments, banks, credit card companies, fast-food restaurant, and others are expressing interest in seeing the use of smart cards on a large scale. However, issues of privacy, security, and authentication will need to be addressed before the widespread use of cards capable of carrying everything from cash to vital statistics is generally accepted by the pubic.

99. What is true of 'smart cards'?

(A) They have magnetic stripes.

(B) They were invented in Europe.

(C) They can be connected to the Internet.

(D) They use microchips to store information.

100. What concern has been raised about the use of 'smart cards'?

(A) They can be easily erased.

(B) It may be dangerous to have personal and financial information on one card.

(C) It will be more difficult for governments to collect taxes on electronic transactions.

(D) People may be tempted to spend more electronically than they would using hard cash.

101. What is true of magnetic stripes?

    (A) Some are smaller than a fingernail.

    (B) They have more than 80 separate sections.

    (C) They can be recharged almost indefinitely.

    (D) They hold less information than microchips.

102. What would some companies like to see happen with 'smart cards'?

    (A) Improvements in memory

    (B) Integration with cellular telephones

    (C) Adaptations for u se on the Internet

    (D) Ability to transfer money between bank accounts

During his campaign for Congress, a candidate received a call from one of his campaign managers. "Look, Jim," he said. "You've got to go to Dallas and make a speech. The opposition is telling some lies about you over there."

"I'd like to," Jim said. "But I've got to go to Houston."

"But, Jim," his manager said, "they're telling lies about you in Dallas."

"Yeah," Jim said. "But they're telling the truth about me in Houston."

Surf's Up!

A recent survey has shown what many have long suspected: that the internet as a business tool may actually be counterproductive. The survey found that the internet was perceived as useful by only 35 percent of respondents and in fact many companies with Internet access do not use it because employees aimlessly 'surf the net' rather than do productive work.

The Internet is a world-wide network of computers linked by telephone lines, bringing about, in theory, an unprecedented exchange of information between buyers and sellers.

"While Internet hardware and service providers continue to rave about the Internet revolutionizing business and personal communications, the reality is that it may actually be responsible for decreasing overall productivity," aid Walter Marvin, chief executive of Technology Assessment Incorporated, the survey's organizer.

103. Why are some companies not using their Internet access?

(A) Rising costs have made it expensive to use.

(B) They have found it is not useful for selling their products.

(C) Employees often use it to waste time instead of performing their jobs.

(D) Employees lack the skills and training to make productive use of it.

104. According to Mr. Marvin, what do Internet service providers claim?

(A) The use of the Internet improves businesses.

(B) The Internet may decrease worker productivity.

(C) The Internet will revolutionize productivity of workers.

(D) The technology revolution will soon make today's businesses outdated.

TREEVIEW ESTATES

127 Brookline Road, Nokesville, VA

MEMORANDUM

To   : Sales Agents
From   : Jack Parville, President
Date   : May 2, 19--
Subject : April Housing Sales

The statistics for April housing sales are in, and show the market gaining strength. Last month's sales of 85 units is an increase of over 20% from last month, and up more than 30% from a year ago. Most of the improvement comes from the influx of new workers at the Moore Brothers Cement plant, which is set to begin production on June first. April interest rates, at or near 7.2% for most of the month, have also helped sales. However, there are signs that rates will begin to climb gradually over the next few months, so agents may want to stress to customers the advantages of purchasing now. A more complete presentation on April sales will be made during the next staff meeting, but the preliminary data suggest that the market continues to be strongest for starter homes, those under $150,000, and weakest at prices above $275,000.

105. What is one reason for the increase in April housing sales?

(A) A new cement plant will be opening soon.

(B) A flood in February destroyed many houses.

(C) Banks are offering special deals to first—time home buyers.

(D) Treeview Estates has offered discounts to anyone who buys during April or May.

106. How do April's sales compare to those from April of a year previous?

(A) They have increased by 7.2%

(B) They are up by over 20%

(C) They have increased by more than 30%

(D) They have nearly doubled.

107. What is expected to happen to interest rates?

(A) They will remain stable

(B) They will slowly increase.

(C) They will decline gradually.

(D) They will increase to 7.2%

108. What is true of homes priced at over $275,000?

(A) They do not sell well.

(B) More than 30 units were sold in April.

(C) They are the most popular selling units.

(D) They were available at a discount in April.

During his campaign for Congress, a candidate received a call from one of his campaign managers. "Look, Jim," he said. "You've got to go to Dallas and make a speech. The opposition is telling some lies about you over there."

"I'd like to," Jim said. "But I've got to go to Houston."

"But, Jim," his manager said, "they're telling lies about you in Dallas."

"Yeah," Jim said. "But they're telling the truth about me in Houston."

FAX COVER SHEET
Number of pages (including this cover) : 7

To : Derek Stemple   Tel : 275-0978   Fax : 275-09880
From : Gary Shea   Tel : 843-8567   Fax : 843-7203
Date : 15 November 19--
Message :
Derek,

As we arranged earlier on the phone, I'm sending copies of the contract for developing a second series of textbooks. It is substantially different from the first contract and I'd like your opinion on it -- especially clauses 9 and 10 on the second page. They seem to indicate that I would not be entitled to any royalties for foreign publication. Is this standard? I have some reservations about signing it and would like to discuss it with you, once you have had time to go over it. I appreciate your offer to help me with this matter and look forward to talking with you at your earliest convenience.

Sincerely,

Gary

---

109. Why has this message been written?

(A) To arrange a meeting with Mr. Stemple

(B) To request an additional copy of a book

(C) To ask Mr. Shea to send a copy of his contract

(D) To indicate that additional pages are being sent

110. What does Mr. Shea hesitate to do?

(A) Sign a new contract

(B) Have his books published abroad

(C) Pay royalties on any books sold abroad

(D) Discuss the details of his business negotiations

111. What does Mr. Shea want Mr. Stemple to do?

(A) Provide advice on a contract

(B) Write a new series of textbooks

(C) Arrange a meeting with the publisher

(D) Make hotel reservations for the 9th and 10th

A drunk was walking down the street with both his ears blistered, and he met a friend who asked what happened. "My wife left her hot iron out by the phone when she left the room," said the drunkard. "The phone rang and I picked up the iron by mistake."

"But what about the other ear?"

"The s.o.b called back!"

A Wet weekend at the Races

The Santa Lucia Yacht Club is proud to announce its Fifth Annual Maritime Races this weekend, April 8 &9, at the City Harbor Club. As in the past, the event is co-sponsored by The Santa Lucia Yacht Club and the Harbor Masters' League. Presiding as chief judge at this year's races is Admiral Robert Clearwater, formerly the Commander of the USS Intrepid Other judges will include local entertainers and sports celebrities.

To register for the event, you must bring a photo ID as well as a maritime license approved by the Harbor Masters' League. This year the competition will be separated into two divisions, amateur and professional; however, all contestants must have at least two years of sailing experience.

Prizes will be awarded to the top two finishers of each division. Amateur sailors must register no later than Thursday, April 6, and professional sailors by Friday, April 7.

There will be plenty of parking available for spectators, and refreshments will be provided by the Association of Harbor Restaurants.

Check your local listings for race times.

---

112. Who are the official supporters of the Maritime Races?

(A) Admiral Robert Clearwater and the other judges

(B) The Santa Lucia Yacht Club and the

(C) The Santa Lucia Yacht Club and the Harbor Masters' League

(D) The Santa Lucia Yacht Club and The

113. Who can register to compete in the event?

(A) Only professional seamen

(B) Only the sailors of the USS Intrepid sailing experience

(C) Anyone with a couple of years of sailing experience

(D) Anyone who enjoys weekend sailing

114. By when must professional sailors register?

(A) No later than April 6

(B) Between April 6 and April 7

(C) No later than April 7

(D) After April 6

115. For whom is this advertisement intended?

(A) Anyone interested in sailing

(B) People who need parking spaces during the weekend

(C) Members of the Santa Lucia Yacht

(D) Anyone interested in learning how to sail

A man was in a grocery store with his stingy friend when two robbers stormed in and announced a stick up. As the robbers began searching the patrons for money, the man felt a nudge. "Take this," his pal whispered. "Don't give me a gun," the man whispered back. "I don't want to be a hero." "It's not a gun, it's that twenty-five dollars I owe you"

MORE COFFEE ANYONE?

For the past two centuries, the coffee growers of Spanish Anguilla have resided in the country's lush mountains, patiently growing the best coffee beans in the world.

Each grower owns not more than thirty acres of land for his endeavor, and some growers own as little as five acres each. Thus, each coffee plant is assured of receiving the best individual care it possibly can, and each coffee bean retains its pure, natural taste.

The growing process is a long arduous one. Nevertheless. because each coffee farm is passed down from generation to generation within families, the secrets of coffee growing remain intact. There are no recorded procedures nor any literature about harvesting methods. Simply put, evert Anguillan grower knows his coffee.

Yet, modern methods have infiltrated this quiet industry with new technological advances aimed at increasing output. And although the amount of Anguillan coffee has gone up, the quality of the coffee has not followed the trend. Instead. modern tampering has had an opposite effect on the quality of Anguillan coffee.

---

116. What is the purpose of this passage?

(A) To explain the methods of coffee production in Anguilla

(B) To show how the coffee farmers of Anguilla live

(C) To demonstrate how each generation of coffee growers produce coffee plants

(D) To describe Anguillan coffee and state the negative effect of technology in the Anguillan coffee industry

117. According to the passage, for what reason is Anguillan coffee of such good quality?

(A) Each farmer grows his plants without keeping any records

(B) Each farmer maintains a small farm so that he can give great care to each plant

(C) Each farmer develops different types of coffee beans so that there are different coffee flavors

(D) Each farmer receives a pension from the Anguillan government

118. What is the author's main concern?

(A) Technology is assuring the production of more Anguillan coffee but reducing its quality

(B) Without written accounts, the secrets of coffee growing may be lost

(C) Technology will ruin the land used to grow coffee, therefore driving the coffee farmers out from a way of life

(D) Anguillan coffee will no longer be produced in such mass quantities

At a department store, a difficult customer and a patient clerk were having a hard time getting together. Nothing the clerk provided was exactly what the woman wanted. finally, the finicky shopper said in annoyance, "Can't you find a smarter clerk to serve me?"

"No." said the saleswoman. "The smarter clerk saw you coming and disappeared."

Questions *119 – 122* are based on the following article.

What Does it Take to Get a Job?

Most normal people get very nervous just before an interview. After all, how you perform in the next half hour or so could mean the difference between getting a job and having to go on more interviews. Well, here are some tips on how to show your best side.

First, start off with a positive attitude. Believe that you already have the job; the interview is just an orientation. That's right. The security of thinking that you have the job in question will relax you, making you feel less anxious and allowing you speak fluidly in the face of the interviewer.

Next, make sure you look presentable. And that doesn't mean overdoing yourself on the ornaments. For men, a watch is fine. No bracelets or other excessive jewelry. For women, one item around the neck. And no excessive make-up. Remember too much is bad. On the other hand, too little is bad, also. Make sure you wear clean, pressed, business attire. This means no blue-jeans and no T-shirts.

Finally, wipe your hands. You don't want the first impression to be overshadowed by the presence of sweaty palms. Now, go get that job.

---

119. Why was this passage written?

(A) It shows people how to dress for their jobs

(B) It demonstrates the effectiveness of positive thinking

(C) It explains how to conduct an interview

(D) It gives advice on what to do before an interview

120. According to the author, what is the effect of thinking the job is already yours?

(A) It is psychologically proven to help you relax in these situations

(B) It speeds up heart-rate, thereby helping you to think more quickly

(C) It allows you to feel less worry and to speak smoothly

(D) It has no effect whatsoever

121. What is acceptable attire for an interview?

(A) A woman wearing large ear–rings, bright red lipstick, and several necklaces

(B) A woman wearing lots of make–up and a t –shirt and miniskirt

(C) A man wearing blue–jeans and a neck–tie

(D) A man wearing a blue suit

122. How does the author feel abort "sweaty palms"?

(A) It is acceptable to perspire during an interview

(B) Interviewers understand nervousness

(C) A doctor should be consulted to reduce sweating

(D) One should avoid sweaty palms if possible

A party of scholars were going out one day in the holidays to catch rabbits. Among them was one who was singularly devoid of the quality known as common sense, so the others asked him not to talk for fear he should scare the rabbits. But he had no sooner caught sight of a number of rabbits than he called out: "Ecce multi cumiculi," which in English means, Behold many rabbits. Of course the rabbits ran off to their holes, and the sportsmen were disappointed. They scolded their noisy friend, but he innocently answered, "Whoever would have thought that rabbits could understand Latin?"

Notice to Tardy Employees ;

It has come to my attention that many in our staff have taken a liberal interpretation of the company policy concerning punctuality. To these people let me re-iterate this policy: only under extreme circumstances is an employee allowed to be late for work. And I'm sure that each and every one of us knows the definition of "extreme" If you have a good reason for being tardy, make sure you call in advance, informing someone in the office that you will be late.

---

123. Why was this notice given?

    (A) The company policy has changed

    (B) The interpretation of the company policy has been changed

    (C) Many employees have been coming to work late

    (D) Many employees want a change in the company policy

124. What should an employee do if he or she is going to be late to work?

    (A) The employee must explain the situation upon arrival

    (B) The employee should apologize to the rest of the staff

    (C) The employee must give a written account of his or her reasons

    (D) The employee should phone the office before arrival

At a grand Christmas party, a young man asked an attractive elderly lady for a dance. "Sorry, I don't dance with a baby." refused the lady. The young man challenged, "Sorry, I didn't know you are pregnant."

COLD TURKEY

Millions of people around the world are addicted to cigarette smoking. For them smoking is a bad habit difficult to break. Everyone knows the harm smoking can do, not only to the smokers themselves, but also to those around them, There are dozens of products on the market that can help a smoker quit. They range from nicotine gum to acupuncture treatments. However, if you're like the many thousands of people who have tried these products, you know that none of them will help you stop smoking. So what's the answer to cigarette smoking?

According to a panel of doctors who specialize in curing addictions, the best way to stop cigarette smoking, as with any addiction, is to simply STOP COLD TURKEY. That's right. The best way to stop cigarette smoking is to just stop, without the aid of any products. And it can be done at any time, the sooner the better. All of the products out on the market are only temporary cures for the addiction known as smoking. Even if you actually did stop smoking by using those products, you would most likely go back to smoking within six months. So why waste your money on gimmicks? Give this age-old method a try. Give your will-power a try.

125. What is the purpose of this passage?

(A) It is advertising a new product which cures cigarette smoking

(B) It denounces several products that guarantee that the user will stop smoking

(C) It is advertising a new brand of cigarettes that help cure smoking

(D) It recommends that the surest way to stop smoking is to simply stop

126. According to the author, how many products will actually help people to stop smoking?

(A) Only acupuncture treatments

(B) Only a few products on the market

(C) No product on the market

(D) Only those recommended by doctors

127. When is the best time to quit smoking?

(A) Within six months

(B) After trying all or most of the products out on the market

(C) After consulting a doctor

(D) As soon as possible

128. According to the author, what does "COLD TURKEY" mean?

(A) It is a brand new way to stop smoking

(B) It is a medical term for rare birds of flight

(C) It means that one should rely on oneself to overcome addictions

(D) It is a new product for smokers which relies on age-old formulas that will help the user overcome cigarette smoking

129. Why does the author think "COLD TURKEY" is a benefit to those who decide to use it?

(A) It is free and it works

(B) It takes effect after only six months

(C) It is good for people who cannot afford expensive products

(D) It works only for those people who have tried other products

Questions *130 - 133* are based on the following report.

Do You Speak English?

The study of English as a second language has been popular for many years, and with the growth of a world economy there has been a great surge in English study. As many smaller nations enter the global economic scene, particularly in Asia, their industries have found it necessary and crucial to teach employees the English language.

A case in point is South Korea. Today, almost all companies have a language program in which the employees must learn English for advancement. Some firms have in-house programs where employees are taught by fluent English speaking colleagues, and others send their employees to independent language institutions. These language institutions are the result of the popularity of the English language, and in most Asian nations they have become a separate and highly profitable industry.

It appears that although the study of English began as a prerequisite foradvancement in global economics. it has also branched off into its own niche within this same vast arena.

---

130. According to the passage, how long has English been popular as a second language?

(A) Its popularity has just begun

(B) Its has been popular for quite a number of years

(C) It has been popular since the Korean War.

(D) It has always been popular

131. All of the following statements are supported by the author, except:

(A) English is popular in smaller countries

(B) English is popular in industrial companies

(C) English is popular in South Korea

(D) English language training has been successful in most companies

132. What are some ways in which companies teach English to their employees?

(A) Training within the company and by instruction outside of the companies

(B) Training within the company and through night classes at universities

(C) Interactive group studies between colleagues and competitors

(D) Home studies with fluent speaking colleagues

133. What is the result of English's popularity?

(A) The study of English has become quite easier

(B) There has been an increase in global economics

(C) There are no tangible results

(D) The study of English has arisen as an industry in itself

Answering an ad for employment, a young student arrived early for an interview, but found several applicants ahead of him. He wrote a quick note and handed it to the receptionist, telling her it was important that her boss receive the note at once. She smiled as she read it, then took it to the boss. "Dear Sir," the note read. "I am tenth in line. Please don't make any decision until you've interviewed me."

He got the jod.

Questions *134 - 136* are based on the following memo.

Weather Forecast

The following forecast gives information on weather from Sunday, December 10th to Saturday, December 16th.

Expect mild winter temperatures during the first half of the week. Mornings will still be chilly, but afternoons will be getting warmer- with bright sunshine at least until Wednesday. Then, beginning Thursday, a cold front will move in and freezing temperatures can be expected for the rest of the week with an 80% chance of snow on Friday and Saturday.

For more details concerning the weather, please check the map on the last page of the finance section.

---

134. What is the duration of the forecast?

    (A) The winter season

    (B) The holiday season

    (C) The month of December

    (D) One week in December

135. What does the article say about the weather?

    (A) It will remain constant and fair

    (B) It is unpredictable

    (C) It will snow during the first part of the week

    (D) It will change as the week progresses

136. Where can further in formation be obtained?

    (A) In the weekend edition

    (B) In the evening paper

    (C) In the Finance section

    (D) On television

Questions *137 - 138* are based on the following announcement.

An Error

The November 10th edition of The New England Herald, sports section, erroneously printed that baketball star Kevin O' Neal would wed Christine Jackson of Minmoth, Ohio. Instead, the sports figure will exchange nuptial vows with mega-model Christine Johnson on November 29th.

We apologize to Mr. O' Neal and Ms. Johnson for the error.

kevin jackson.

Editor in Chief, The New England Herald

137. When did this notice appear?

(A) On November 10th

(B) On November 29th

(C) After the wedding

(D) There is not enough information given

138. Why was this notice given?

(A) The newspaper mistakenly printed that Kevin O' Neal would divorce Ms. Jackson

(B) The newspaper printed that Kevin O' Neal would divorce Ms. Johnson

(C) The newspaper mistakenly printed that Kevin O' Neal would marry Ms. Jackson

(D) The newspaper would like to congratulate the two participants

This Software Does Everything

Soft-Comp proudly introduces its new line of software : Mini-Byte System, for the home or the office. The system contains over fifteen separate products for all of your filing needs. It can handle the affairs of an average household of four, or can run the business of the small company. The system does the work of three administrative assistants. It files, it edits, it faxes, it makes copies, it answers telephones··· the only thing it doesn't do is make coffee!

For a free consultation by one of our knowledge sales representatives, call Soft-Comp now. 1-800-SOFTCOMP. Or, if you're familiar with our line of products, and would like to order, call 1-800-SOFTBUY. Operators are standing by.

139. What is being advertised?

(A) Software for family accounting

(B) Computers for small businesses

(C) Computers for households and small businesses

(D) Software for households and offices

140. Which task is not mentioned as something the Mini-Byte can perform?

(A) Answer telephones

(B) Arrange files

(C) Produce refreshments

(D) Arrange paperwork

> Overhearing my husband and me making plans for a weekend trip, our 16-year-old daughter announced that she wanted to stay home alone. Upon getting our negative reaction, she pleaded, "Why can't I? You used to say no because I was too young, but now-"
>
> "Now," interrupted her father, "you're too old."

모범 답안

1	Ⓓ	2	Ⓒ	3	Ⓓ	4	Ⓒ	5	Ⓑ	6	Ⓒ	7	Ⓑ	8	Ⓓ	9	Ⓐ	10	Ⓒ
11	Ⓑ	12	Ⓓ	13	Ⓓ	14	Ⓑ	15	Ⓓ	16	Ⓒ	17	Ⓐ	18	Ⓐ	19	Ⓑ	20	Ⓒ
21	Ⓐ	22	Ⓓ	23	Ⓑ	24	Ⓒ	25	Ⓓ	26	Ⓒ	27	Ⓑ	28	Ⓒ	29	Ⓒ	30	Ⓑ
31	Ⓑ	32	Ⓐ	33	Ⓑ	34	Ⓓ	35	Ⓑ	36	Ⓒ	37	Ⓑ	38	Ⓐ	39	Ⓒ	40	Ⓑ
41	Ⓓ	42	Ⓑ	43	Ⓑ	44	Ⓓ	45	Ⓐ	46	Ⓓ	47	Ⓑ	48	Ⓒ	49	Ⓑ	50	Ⓓ
51	Ⓒ	52	Ⓐ	53	Ⓓ	54	Ⓓ	55	Ⓐ	56	Ⓑ	57	Ⓒ	58	Ⓒ	59	Ⓑ	60	Ⓑ
61	Ⓐ	62	Ⓑ	63	Ⓐ	64	Ⓒ	65	Ⓓ	66	Ⓐ	67	Ⓒ	68	Ⓐ	69	Ⓑ	70	Ⓑ
71	Ⓐ	72	Ⓓ	73	Ⓐ	74	Ⓒ	75	Ⓒ	76	Ⓒ	77	Ⓐ	78	Ⓑ	79	Ⓓ	80	Ⓒ
81	Ⓓ	82	Ⓐ	83	Ⓓ	84	Ⓐ	85	Ⓐ	86	Ⓒ	87	Ⓒ	88	Ⓓ	89	Ⓒ	90	Ⓐ
91	Ⓑ	92	Ⓑ	93	Ⓐ	94	Ⓒ	95	Ⓒ	96	Ⓑ	97	Ⓑ	98	Ⓒ	99	Ⓓ	100	Ⓑ
101	Ⓓ	102	Ⓒ	103	Ⓒ	104	Ⓐ	105	Ⓐ	106	Ⓒ	107	Ⓑ	108	Ⓐ	109	Ⓓ	110	Ⓐ
111	Ⓐ	112	Ⓒ	113	Ⓒ	114	Ⓒ	115	Ⓐ	116	Ⓓ	117	Ⓑ	118	Ⓐ	119	Ⓓ	120	Ⓒ
121	Ⓓ	122	Ⓓ	123	Ⓒ	124	Ⓑ	125	Ⓓ	126	Ⓒ	127	Ⓓ	128	Ⓒ	129	Ⓐ	130	Ⓑ
131	Ⓓ	132	Ⓐ	133	Ⓓ	134	Ⓓ	135	Ⓓ	136	Ⓒ	137	Ⓓ	138	Ⓒ	139	Ⓓ	140	Ⓒ

토익 토플 R/C

2011년 3월 2일 초판1쇄 인쇄
2011년 3월 5일 초판1쇄 발행

저 자 최 우 순
펴낸이 임 순 재

펴낸곳 **한올출판사**

등록 제11-403호
① ② ① - ⑧ ④ ⑨
주 소 서울시 마포구 성산동 133-3 한올빌딩 3층
전 화 (02)376-4298(대표)
팩 스 (02)302-8073
홈페이지 www.hanol.co.kr
e-메 일 hanol@hanol.co.kr
정 가 **13,000원**

저자와의
협의하에
인지생략